Disclaimer: The opinions presented herein are solely those of the author except where specifically noted. Nothing in the book should be construed as investment advice or guidance, as it is not intended as investment advice or guidance, nor is it offered as such. Nothing in the book should be construed as a recommendation to buy or sell any financial or physical asset. It is solely the opinion of the writer, who is not an investment professional. The strategies presented in the book may be unsuitable for you, and you should consult a professional where such consultation is appropriate. The publisher/author disclaims any implied warranty or applicability of the contents for any particular purpose. The publisher/author shall not be liable for any commercial or incidental damages of any kind or nature.

First ebook edition published July 2011
First print edition published September 2011

Oftwominds.com
P.O. Box 4727
Berkeley, California 94704

An Unconventional Guide to Investing in Troubled Times

Charles Hugh Smith

With gratitude to Harun Ibrahim, Stewart J. Pillette (1938 – 2009) and Cindy N. Furukawa, without whose help and insights this book could not have been written.

Table of Contents

Introduction

Introduction

As I write this in mid- 2011, the financial world seems remarkably resilient: global markets have shrugged off oil climbing above $100 per barrel, chain-reaction rebellions in North Africa and the Mideast, a devastating earthquake and tsunami in northeast Japan, rising food and energy costs, a sovereign debt crisis in Europe and a decline in the U.S. dollar to multi-year lows.

Despite these systemic risks, the U.S. stock markets have climbed back to their 2008 pre-financial crisis levels. The mainstream financial media is again touting reasons why stocks will continue rising: the recovery is now self-sustaining, inflation remains low, corporate profits, already at record levels, will keep levitating higher, and the Federal Reserve has pledged to keep interest rates near zero indefinitely.

"Don't fight the Fed" has entered the investment lexicon as an iron law of nature akin to gravity. The Fed's quantitative easing policy, designed to lower the U.S. dollar and ignite inflation, has richly rewarded buyers of risk assets such as stocks and commodities.

With the market up over 100% since the March 2009 lows and corporate profits exceeding pre-crisis levels, the sky is once again the limit. Financial authorities routinely present projections out to 2030 and beyond, confident that government budgets and global markets will remain stable for decades to come.

It's truly as if the 2008 global financial crisis never happened. All is right with the world once again. Indeed, the market's "discounting of bad news" seems like a replay of the Bull Markets of 1987, 1997 and 2007.

But behind this façade of recovery, the fundamental dynamics have changed. The financial firestorm of 2008 that was apparently extinguished by unprecedented central bank interventions is still smoldering. Only the amount of deadwood—the excesses of risk, debt and leverage that led to near-collapse in 2008—have piled even higher.

The monetary and fiscal "fixes" imposed by authorities around the globe since 2008 didn't reduce the global financial system's instability, they merely suppressed outward signs of instability. Beneath this tranquil surface, the "fixes" have greatly increased the global financial system's instability. Like an apparently peaceful forest filled with dry deadwood, a single spark can ignite a new firestorm that will burn with greater ferocity and speed than the financial fire of 2008.

This instability is beyond the reach of the regulatory "medicine" that has been offered as a cure; it is systemic, the consequence of profound structural imbalances in global demographics, resource consumption, debt, leverage, risk and governance. Behind the facade, the world's financial systems are increasingly precarious, as a key feature of systemic instability is that small, unpredictable fluctuations can trigger outsized consequences.

This instability naturally creates anxiety and fear, as we all have much to lose in the next financial firestorm. We fear what we don't understand. This book is based on a simple but profound idea: that the best way to conquer fear and anxiety is to understand the world's financial instability at the deepest levels. Understanding is empowering. To this end, the book presents a great many ideas, some of which may be familiar to you and some which may be unfamiliar. Since we learn by having ideas presented in different forms, the book will occasionally test the patience of those readers to whom this is all familiar.

The acceleration of change in our digitized world has shortened investment timelines down to months or weeks for investors and minutes or seconds for high-frequency trading machines. This compression of time has made us impatient for answers. The trends and dynamics described in this book will take years to fully play out, so a longer view is required.

When we face risk, complacency and false hope are great dangers. To believe that the Status Quo will endure without any real changes being needed is a false hope. This book offers an alternative perspective, one that views troubled times as a great opportunity for those prepared for change. Our ideas of capital and wealth will be challenged, but in a positive way. In this sense, I believe this book will be inspirational to all who prefer the truth to complacency and false hope.

In an analogy many of us can relate to, this choice is similar to a doctor's diagnosis and treatment options for a chronic disease: do we want empty reassurances that "everything will be fine," when we know in our bones that everything is not at all fine, or do we want the plain truth, including the uncertainties that come with a realistic assessment? Reassurances and complacency appeal to our desire for normalcy, but deep down we know we cannot possibly get better without hearing the truth about our condition and the pros and cons of various treatment options. Only when we know these can we take charge of our own lives and destinies.

SECTION ONE
Systemic Risk and Investing

1 | An Overview of Instability

1) What was once considered "impossible" has been normalized to the point that truly unprecedented imbalances are now accepted as "normal." But the normalcy is illusory.

For example, it is now considered "normal" that the Federal government borrows $1.6 trillion every year to prop up the Status Quo, fully 11% of America's Gross Domestic Product (GDP) and 40% of all Federal expenditures. This stands in stark contrast to the traditional view that deficits in excess of 3% of GDP a year are inherently destabilizing. Now we borrow roughly four times that much (including the off-budget "supplemental appropriations" that run into the hundreds of billions of dollars every year) and the political and financial Elites evince a complacent faith that these extremes are benign and sustainable.

Those who believe unprecedented central bank and State interventions in global markets are not just necessary but positive point to Japan, a nation that thus far is untroubled by debts far in excess of 200% of its GDP. They also point to the rapid growth in developing countries as the engine which will grow the world's financial pie so everyone's slice gets bigger every year.

But the fundamental problems in the global economy have not been addressed--they've just been papered over with trillions of dollars in printed or borrowed money. Behind the paper-thin façade of "extend and pretend" normalcy, the foundations of the financial Status Quo in China, Japan, the European Union and the U.S. rest on shifting sand. By avoiding structural reform in favor of facsimiles of reform and by "fixing" over-indebtedness with more debt, the political and financial Elites have simply increased the height the world will have to fall to correct the imbalances.

In the forest fire analogy, fixing debt crises by adding more debt is like putting out a small fire: that suppression of a healthy cleansing of the system only guarantees a monstrous fire later.

2) The global economy is now based on a widespread trust that central banks and governments will never let assets fall in value. This insulation from risk is known as moral hazard, as those who are insulated from risk will have an insatiable appetite for risky bets because any gains will be theirs to keep but any losses will be covered by the central bank.

The financial authorities' success in propping up assets like stocks in the U.S. and real estate in China over the past three years has strengthened this moral hazard into a dangerous quasi-religious faith that central banks and governments have essentially unlimited power to keep asset prices aloft via printing money and easy credit.

3) This isn't just a failure to reform an opaque and broken financial system: conventional economics has failed. This Grand Failure of Conventional Economics has gone unnoticed, as all those wedded to the Status Quo keep applying "lessons learned" during The Great Depression of the 1930s. They are pursuing the magical-thinking hope that the old rules still apply, even though the fundamentals have changed dramatically.

The Grand Failure of Conventional Economics is more than failed policy: it is a profound blindness to the resource limitations of our planet. Not one of the many strands of conventional economics recognizes the limits on growth in production and consumption as measured by GDP (Gross Domestic Product).

When the planet's human population reached 500 million, there were sufficient resources to enable a doubling to 1 billion. Then 1 billion tripled to 3 billion, which has doubled to 6 billion. Now, as China, India and other nations are industrializing, the 600 million high-consumption "middle class" of the developed economies is expanding four-fold to 2.4 billion.

There simply isn't enough oil and other resources on the planet, in any remotely plausible scenario, for 600 million of China's 1.3 billion people to live on an American scale of consumption, not to mention 600 million of India's 1.2 billion, and another billion avid consumers in other developing economies.

4) Conventional economics is also incapable of grasping the profound consequences of disruptive technologies that are "creatively destroying" the old foundations of centralized economies and replacing them with decentralized models of much greater efficiency. These new technologies are resistant to controls imposed by concentrations of power such as central banks and governments. Centralization—what I call the "factory" model—reaped enormous gains in the industrialization era; now centralization is increasingly counter-productive, as coordinated monetary manipulations have destabilized the global economy.

Industries that were once mainstays of the economy have been destroyed by irresistibly efficient Internet, communications and digital technologies: long-distance telephony, travel agencies, musical recordings, print media and retailing, to name a few. Next to be disrupted: education, healthcare, finance and government, precisely those industries widely considered immune to creative destruction.

5) These forces are incomprehensible to conventional economics partly because they are triggering simultaneous effects such as deflation and inflation which have been understood as linear and sequential. Disruption of old industries is deflationary to price and employment even as massive government money printing and support of moral hazard is inflationary. As "hot money" flees old industries and seeks higher returns from speculation, asset bubbles expand and pop as capital is misallocated into overcapacity. As money is devalued by these monetary policies, bizarre analogs of money such as derivatives, mortgage-backed securities and tulip bulbs arise and then implode in what I term the speculative supernova model.

6) This dynamic intersection of disruptive new decentralizing technologies, resource depletion and the grand failure of conventional economics is unprecedented in human history; we would have to look back to the era that was transformed by the invention of the printing

press, the explosive rise of Renaissance commerce and the discovery of the New World for historical precedents. The difference is the accelerated pace of transformation in our digital era: changes that took 200 years to unfold between 1500 and 1700 will likely be compressed into the next 20 years. The predictability of this process of creative destruction is low; nobody knows what will happen five years hence, much less 20 years hence.

Francis Bacon wrote in 1620 that the printing press "changed the whole face and state of things throughout the world." The same can be said of the Internet and other digital technologies, and the transformation of the global economy is far from complete.

7) From the long view, conventional economics developed in the era of ever-cheaper, ever-more abundant energy and the miraculous "low hanging fruit" productivity gains made possible by cheap energy and centralized mass production. Like a creature born in the morning that has only seen daylight, conventional economics has never experienced night and so it has no conception of darkness.

Thus the current failure of conventional economics is not the failure of individuals or policies--it is a profound conceptual failure. Conventional economics, based on limitless "growth," globalized financialization, and ever-greater central bank-Central State intervention in markets, is incapable of understanding a world of resource limits and a financial system that is increasingly vulnerable to unpredictable cascades.

Behind the present rose-tinted façade, the only limitless resources are paper money and propaganda. Everything else is limited by real world constraints. An economy that consumes ever-greater quantities of real-world resources such as oil, and harvests renewable resources such as timber and wild fisheries at rates far in excess of their renew rates, will soon encounter shortages and higher prices as those with paper or electronic money bid for the remaining reserves.

8) The markets now depend on massive State and central bank intervention for their veneer of stability. The "ratchet effect" is in full force:

every crisis requires ever greater State borrowing and ever larger interventions by central banks. If this vast machinery of intervention were withdrawn, the system's fundamental instability would be revealed.

This intervention is not limited to monetary policy; official statistics have been gamed to support the Status Quo assertions of a return to prosperity. This legerdemain has two unintended consequences: it discredits the statistics and the government that issues them, and it undermines market correlations that had been valid for decades. Investors and speculators alike are rushing to the lifeboats to find they're only paper mache stage props.

9) The human mind has a number of default settings which have proven advantageous as "short cuts" in most circumstances, one of which is called "the normalcy bias." As events spiral out of control and dangers rise exponentially, our tendency is to underestimate the risks and potential losses. As long as a few shreds of normalcy remain intact, we view these as evidence that "it's really not so bad."

Most of the time, this trait pays off as most systems are self-correcting and catastrophe is avoided. But when self-reinforcing negative trends take hold, this complacency is ultimately self-destructive.

10) The financial Status Quo, already discredited in the eyes of most well-informed observers, will eventually lose all credibility, and global stock markets will languish as participants abandon them.

If this sounds farfetched, recall that 70% of all shares traded in the U.S. stock market are exchanged in opaque "dark pools" operated by Wall Street and "too big to fail" banks, and high-frequency trading executed by "black box" algorithms account for the majority of the remaining 30% of publicly traded shares. This means that some 90% of stock market activity is hidden from non-insider investors.

The idea that we can rely on opaque markets for our financial security will increasingly be discredited. As heavy-handed interventions fail to restore stability, public faith in these institutions will decline. This delegitimization will further destabilize global markets, and those who accepted the implicit guarantees of stability, transparency and liquidity may find instead that their financial security has vanished in a cloud of "impossible" disruptions and dislocations.

This loss of faith is already evident. As the U.S. stock market doubled from its March 2009 lows, U.S. households withdrew hundreds of billions of dollars from domestic equity mutual funds, and quadrupled their holdings of "safe" U.S. Treasury bonds. If you look at a 10-year chart of volume in U.S. stocks, you will see a steady erosion of participation in the stock market. These are the actions of people who have lost faith in the stock market, the nation's financial and political institutions and the official "story" of permanently rising prosperity.

Once trust is lost, it cannot be won back easily or quickly.

As the financial authorities attempt to keep the system from crumbling beneath their feet, they will take increasingly drastic actions as markets destabilize: investment rules that were presumed to be eternal will be changed overnight, without warning, and then changed again. Decades of low volatility that encouraged people to buy long-term bonds, annuities and dividend-paying stocks will be upended by unprecedented financial and political volatility. Seemingly permanent low interest rates that lured investors to pile into high-risk gambles will suddenly leap up, wiping out gamblers who weren't even aware they were playing a game rigged in favor of the "house."

Such expectations are well-grounded in history. Most investors have forgotten that the U.S. stock market was summarily closed for months during World War I, and that in 1933, the Federal government seized "hoarded" privately held gold. These actions were, at the time, considered necessary and prudent by the authorities. More recently, in 2008 speculating that banking stocks would decline (that is, shorting banking stocks) was summarily banned. The rules governing the market were changed to defend the Status Quo, and speculation was only allowed if it flowed in one direction—the one favored by the financial authorities.

11) Stripped of mumbo-jumbo, central banks and States have only two buttons to push: Keynesian fiscal stimulus, i.e. governments

borrowing and spending vast sums in an effort to stimulate demand and the "animal spirits" that drive private borrowing, and monetary easing, i.e. lowering interest rates to near-zero, and printing or creating credit electronically to flood the economy with "liquid," easy-to-borrow money.

Central banks and States are hitting these two buttons like frenzied laboratory rats, but the machine is out of cocaine-laced pellets. In effect, central banks and Central States are both addicted to exponential expansion of credit, intervention and Central State borrowing and spending. Each is only exacerbating the system's risks, and as the authorities ratchet up these interventions to ever-higher levels, they're insuring an even greater collapse.

There is a pernicious agenda at work in setting interest rates near zero while boosting money supply and deficit spending to create inflation. By robbing savers of any return on their savings and sparking "sustainable, orderly" inflation of around 4%, central banks are in effect transferring 4% from the owners of cash to reduce the debt of the central bank/State by this same amount every year. In a decade of this monetary scheme, savers' wealth will be reduced by roughly 50% while the debt created by the central bank/State will decline by 50%.

"Purchasing power" is a concept while helps us understand the results of low interest rates and "politically benign" inflation: the owner of cash will find their money buys only half of what it did ten years before, while the government debt has also fallen in half. The net result of this slight-of-hand is that government debt that was crushing becomes manageable again as savers' wealth was invisibly transferred via carefully engineered inflation.

The key phrase in this sub rosa agenda of transferring private wealth to reduce government/central bank debt is "politically benign:" since the loss of wealth and the rise in consumer prices is "only" 4% a year, the consequences are not severe enough to trigger political resistance. Financial and political authorities know that people quickly habituate to an "orderly" reduction in wealth and an "orderly" inflation in prices; that is, this erosion of purchasing power soon becomes "the new normal" and people plan around it.

The purpose of this central bank/State agenda is to avoid the two end-games that would destabilize the Status Quo: outright default on the Status Quo's staggering debts, and hyperinflation, or loss of faith in a paper (fiat) currency. Either of these events would destroy the credit markets that form the foundation of the global economy.

We can see how successful this strategy of engineering orderly, "normal" inflation has been: 30 years ago, a Federal debt of $15 trillion would have been unimaginable. Today, it is accepted as "sustainable" because it will never be paid back in today's dollars, and low interest rates insure that the carrying costs of that debt remains small enough that no other government spending need be sacrificed to pay the annual interest.

This agenda has worked like magic for the past 30 years, but beneath the apparent success, the foundations of the current system-- cheap energy, globalization, financialization, monetary expansion, fiscal stimulus, opaque markets and constant State/central bank intervention-- are all eroding. As they dissolve then so too will the Status Quo's implicit promises of permanent stability, low interest rates and limitless growth.

The point here is that the levels of intervention required to create inflation in a deflationary, deleveraging-of-debt era are not just stupendous-- they must ratchet up to ever higher levels to maintain superficial stability as the system becomes increasingly precarious. Ironically, increasing the heavy-handed centralized interventions only increases the system's precariousness—the exact opposite of the Central Planners' intentions. This is the result of trying to manage non-linear systems with linear-system tools: all that manipulation can achieve is to extend surface stability at the cost of a more severe system crash later on.

This poses two challenges for us as investors: if the central banks/States succeed in triggering inflation, how can we maintain our purchasing power? And if they fail to engineer stable inflation, which is increasingly likely, then how do we survive the black hole of hyperinflation or systemic credit default?

12) The Status Quo advice of diversifying your money among global stocks, bonds and commodities may not offer the low risk and security that's being promised, as interconnected global markets are destabilizing in unison.

As we enter this unprecedented era, we quite naturally ask: what can I do to preserve my capital? What can I do to prosper in a tumultuous and increasingly unpredictable world?

13) I am not an economist, money manager or financial advisor—I am an observer. Being an observer offers a number of strengths which I hope to bring to bear in this book. One is a keen awareness that I have no idea what will happen in the future, and neither does anyone else. Nobody knows the price of anything tomorrow, much less its price five years hence.

14) The investment world is keen on probabilities as reliable guides to the future. But low-probability events occur with remarkable regularity, so it's prudent not to put too much faith in statistical or probabilistic reassurances. All such models are based on the idea that the recent past is a reliable guide to the future. But if the thesis that the next 20 years will necessarily be very different from the previous 60 years, then this faith that the recent past offers a roadmap of the future is dangerously misleading.

15) The uneven, unpredictable process of destabilization and devolution will play out over many years as periods of apparent stability are punctuated by the re-emergence of crises which were supposedly resolved in the previous cycle of central bank/government intervention. Every era of stability will be less enduring than the last, and will come to rest at a lower level of security and prosperity than the last. Every intervention will be larger, more desperate and more intrusive than the last, and much less effective.

16) Periods of creative destruction are inherent to Capitalism, indeed, essential to its long-term success. Just as we cannot fool Mother Nature for long--for example, by reckoning we can eliminate forest fires--

we cannot manipulate the global economy to eliminate creative destruction. All the unprecedented efforts of central financial authorities to eliminate risk and instability are simply piling up more deadwood in an already tinderbox forest.

Financial risk is like water in a closed system: it cannot be compressed. As pressure mounts, the risk builds up and eventually escapes, often through whatever part of the system was considered "safe."

Periods of great transition in which existing systems are consumed by creative destruction and a new paradigm emerges offer great opportunities as well as great risks.

If I had to summarize this book in a few sentences, I would say this: Money is a tool; make it work for you. Don't trust Wall Street's false promises; invest with an unblinking eye on systemic risk. Invest in your own life and in the lives of others.

This book explores how to do just that.

(I am indebted to David Gobel, Gary Baker and C.N.F. for some of the ideas presented here.)

2 | Why the Status Quo Is Unsustainable

I find it self-evident that investing decisions made in the 2011-2031 timeframe based on extrapolations of the previous decades will be catastrophically wrong for the simple reason that the next 20 years will have little in common with the past 20 years. Risk and instability will dominate markets everywhere, and the internal forces of destabilization will become increasingly powerful and pervasive. We have reached the end of the 60-year post-war prosperity based on limitless consumption of resources and expansion of credit/debt.

As a result, every assumption that "worked" during the past will be proven catastrophically wrong. Every investment that was once "safe" and "secure" will be revealed as risky and insecure.

The next decade will look less like the boom years of 1982 to 2007— a stable financial platform brimming with speculative opportunities—and more like the French Revolution circa 1789 or perhaps those heady days of 1644 just before the Ming Empire collapsed into a heap.

Consider what happens when a massive expansion of debt is invested in overpriced assets that collapse in value. That is our present and future in a nutshell.

A voluminous literature has already been written to explain why the next 20 years will be unlike the last 20 years. If this concept is new to you, I recommend *The Crash Course* by Chris Martenson, *The Long Emergency* by James Howard Kunstler and *Financial Armageddon* by Michael Panzner.

Why do the coming decades promise to be uniquely troubled? The answer could fill volumes, but here is a condensed version, drawn from my book *Survival+: Structuring Prosperity for Yourself and the Nation*.

There are ten basic dynamics which have undermined the financial Status Quo:

> 1) Extreme concentrations of wealth and political power subvert
> democracy and regulatory oversight

2) Unprecedented demand for finite resources: ecological overshoot, geopolitical competition for dwindling resources

3) Increasing dependence on credit/debt, leverage and financialization, leaving the financial "ecosystem" a centralized monoculture increasingly vulnerable to collapse (i.e. catastrophic loss of diversity)

4) The partnership of corporate cartel Power Elites and the Central State's fiefdoms

5) Mutually reinforcing long-wave cycles of rising prices, debt renunciation and demographics

6) Dependence on systemic financial fraud and opaque State interventions; loss of transparency

7) Reliance on propaganda, manipulated statistics, phony reforms and simulacra fixes

8) Institutional loss of legitimacy, discredited political leadership

9) High fixed costs that feed into each other and resist reduction (the ratchet effect)

10) Creative destruction of mainstay industries and centralized authority by decentralized digital and Internet technologies

While policy changes can temporarily smooth surface instability, the global economy's deeper problems are not so easily addressed; they require an upending of the financial and political Status Quo and new thinking beyond conventional economics. My trading mentor Harun Ibrahim summed up the intrinsic unsustainability of the Status Quo's dependence on exponential increases of credit and consumption in a few devastatingly logical paragraphs:

"Our problems began in 1913 when the Federal Reserve and therefore de facto centralized planning was established. Every generation that ignored the fact that counterfeiting money and lending it at interest is a scheme that has catastrophically failed in all previous attempts deserves what eventually befalls them.

The problem with maintaining inflation at 3% is that it

compounds until the curve approaches vertical. This exponential growth will eventually outpace real productivity and therefore, at some point, fake prosperity has to be created through expansion of credit. What this implies is that what is happening today could have been and probably was predicted well before 1913. But once again politics has trumped reason.

The effects being experienced today had to materialize. Mathematically there is and can be no other outcome. All things being equal, as real productive activity decreased, credit had to be expanded at exponentially increasing rates until exhaustion. Exhaustion occurs at the point where the curve approaches vertical, where infinite credit or money has to be injected infinitely. This is impossible and the reason why all efforts to "save the financial system" thus far have failed.

Credit is being destroyed faster than it can be created.

Those demanding "solutions" do not understand that: 1) The $106 trillion gorilla in the room (i.e. the unfunded entitlements of Social Security and Medicare) cannot be satisfied. What is so egregious is that the Boomer generation saw or should have seen it coming. Instead of tackling a very difficult problem they chose distraction by bread and circuses.

That the most technologically advanced country in history could conceive that sending worthless pieces of paper to China so that they could buy worthless Treasuries so that we could continue to purchase tangible goods that required real human effort and natural resources is either collective insanity, rank stupidity, desperation, or just plain old greed.

Now that we have engaged in this type of activity for decades and the comeuppance is upon us, we demand solutions to avoid the inevitable consequences of ineptitude and apathy.

Means testing will cost billions we do not have, will be implemented ineffectively, and, on scale, will prove ineffective at deflecting the $106 trillion asteroid the size of Rhode Island hurtling at us at a hundred-thousand miles per second.

The situation is untenable. That an insolvent government (starting from a $106 trillion deficit) and facing global peak resource utilization, will somehow effectively manage to administer to a huge retired population with no savings and assets that they will only be able to sell at a loss and pensions denominated in a worthless currency, is at best imprudent.

This Grand Cycle top is unlike any other faced by mankind. We are at peak everything; peak oil; peak food; peak water; peak industrialism; peak credit; but not peak population. There is and will be no excess capacity for growth. The very mechanisms that have allowed *homo sapiens* to reach such high levels of population density are at or near exhaustion.

And there is no Plan B. Those depending on technology to the rescue do not understand that by the time the Trident Submarine was put into production its design was 20 years old -- and obsolete. This type of government performance is not encouraging. Very long term there will be no return to what has become to be known by the Boomer and current generation as status quo.

What will have to happen is a return to using precious resources not for consumerism with all of its

built-in waste (planned obsolescence, disposable
everything) but for producing absolute necessities.

This may all sound grim but if you remove the
adjective, it simply is. Mr. Kunstler's book title cuts to the
heart of the matter -- we have entered a long
emergency."

In essence, expanding the supply of money does not expand the
supply of real-world commodities, which are intrinsically limited. These
include water, soil, minerals and oil. If each of us were given $1 million
tomorrow, prices would quickly rise to the point that one hour of labor—
whatever number is attached to it—would buy the same amount of
tangible goods that it bought before the $1 million expansion in our
personal money supply.

Forty-five years ago in 1966, few would have believed a prediction
that an auto that cost $3,000 would cost $30,000 and a small apartment
that rented for $120 a month would cost $1,200 a month a few decades
hence. Yet that is what has happened. Expanding the supply of money
does not expand the supply of tangible goods, so prices rise to match the
actual surplus value of labor.

The more rapid the expansion of credit and money supply, the more
rapid the price increases to match. This is why many observers view the
present rapid rise in borrowing and money-printing with alarm, as what
took 45 years to accomplish—the loss of most of the U.S. dollar's
purchasing power—could, with the proper acceleration, be repeated in a
few years.

In other words, if we were all able to borrow $1 trillion tomorrow, our
ability to buy tangible goods would not change much, as prices would
quickly jump to the point that it would still take 40 hours of labor to pay a
month's rent, or an hour of labor to buy four loaves of bread, six hours to
buy a barrel of oil, and so on. The purchasing power of our money would
be unchanged, despite the many zeroes added to our money. This is why
counting your wealth in nominal money is so misleading. The only real
measure of money is how many tangible goods can be purchased with it.

If, however, only you and I could borrow $1 trillion into existence, and everyone else was limited in how much they could borrow, then we could exploit this credit-based wealth by trading it for tangible goods. Even though our incomes didn't rise at all, our ability to borrow a stupendous sum of instantly-created money enabled us to leverage a modest income into ownership of a vast array of tangible goods.

Leverage—borrowing a monumental sum of credit from a modest income base—has this magical quality: it enables us to use invented-on-the-spot money with no intrinsic value (i.e. paper or fiat money) to gain control of limited tangible wealth.

This is akin to "fooling Mother Nature:" an illusory form of "wealth" is traded for real wealth. No wonder leverage and debt is so popular; it seems like a magic without any downside.

But there is a downside—actually, two downsides. One is that those who can leverage their incomes via credit first, and at lower rates of interest, have asymmetric advantages over those who must pay higher interest rates or who come late to the credit-binge party.

The housing bubble and bust offers an illustration of this. Those who leveraged their incomes to the hilt in 2000 and bought three homes on speculation at 2000 prices were able to reap outsized gains when they sold the homes to latecomers in 2006. Their highly leveraged credit enabled them to buy tangible goods (homes) which rose in price as others joined the credit-binge party and borrow vast sums to speculate in housing.

As long as incomes rose to match the rising costs of borrowing, or assets rose so that even more debt could be leveraged and then used to pay the costs of borrowing, then all was well. But under the onslaught of essentially limitless leverage (i.e. interest-only, no down payment "stated-income" liar loans) then the housing valuations rose far above historic measures of value.

Housing became the classic credit-fueled "asset bubble," and an example of moral hazard: the gains from participating in the mania accrued to the house flipper, while losses from default and foreclosure would accrue to the lender. As the nominal owner/speculator had "no skin in the game," that is, no down payment to lose, then participation in the game was low-cost and low-risk

Who has first dibs on cheap (low-interest rate) credit? Banks, of course, along with other large financial players, have access to discounted rates from the Federal Reserve and other sources of cheap credit. This gives the financial sector an enormous asymmetric advantage when it comes to leveraging instantly-created credit into ownership of tangible wealth.

Credit has another downside, an insidious characteristic called interest. At first blush, credit enables us to "fool Mother Nature" by buying far more tangible goods than our income would allow. The tradeoff for this leverage is that we pay interest on that borrowed money (debt). As we leverage ever greater sums of debt from the same income, more and more of our earnings is diverted to paying interest.

If income rises as fast as interest payments, then the borrower can keep his head above water. But if incomes stagnate, as they have for 90% of the households in the U.S. for the past 30 years, then eventually these rising interest payments crowd out spending for necessities, and the household can no longer pay the interest. At that point it becomes insolvent and defaults on the debt.

The more we borrow, the greater the future liability in interest payments, and the lower the odds that the principal can be paid off.

For example, a modest purchase of a $500 electronic gadget at consumer-credit rates of interest will, if the principal is never paid off, eventually cost the owner $10,000 in interest payments. Leverage is only a "good deal" at near-zero rates of interest or if the debt is paid off quickly.

The "story" of the U.S. economy over the past 10 years is that we bridged this gap between stagnant income and rising expenses by borrowing unprecedented sums of money, in effect, leveraging the national income. By lowering interest rates, the Federal Reserve enabled the U.S. to "fool Mother Nature" for a few more years. But now that the Fed's rates are near-zero, then lowering rates is no longer a "solution."

We have "fooled Mother Nature" by borrowing more to pay the interest on previous borrowing and to artificially maintain bubble-level asset prices. This has greatly increased our future liabilities and the risk of a collapse in asset values, and thus greatly increased the probabilities of national insolvency.

Put another way: you and I could easily afford a $1 trillion loan each if the loan was offered to us at zero interest. On an interest-only loan, our monthly payment would be zero. In effect, we have each leveraged our modest individual incomes into $1 trillion "war chests" of free money. What sorts of incentives encourage us to risk this "free money" in speculation? After all, there is no way we can pay back the principal if it is lost, so the incentives overwhelmingly favor speculation: any gains we reap will be ours to keep, while losses will be absorbed by the lender should we default.

This is the defining characteristic of moral hazard: a person insulated from risk will have an appetite for extremely risky bets that those who are not insulated would rationally view as foolhardy.

Distilled down, this is the "story" of the U.S. economy, and beneath the phony reforms and endless bailouts of private losses by the government (i.e. taxpayers), nothing has changed. We continue to "fool Mother Nature" with ever-rising borrowing and leverage, and super-low interest rates have enabled us to continue playing the game as if the future costs of that debt won't inevitably lead to insolvency.

We tend to speak of leverage in financial terms, but as Harun observed, leverage and thus risk is ever-present in everything from oil to technology:

> "Some call it complexity or hyper-complexity, but to me it's all about leverage. The greater the leverage, the greater the instability, and developed societies are heavily leveraged in technology (knowledge), finance (credit) and energy. Remember, your prediction of a 4%

failure rate in home mortgages causing a complete
collapse in that sector was dead on. But that 4%, which
globally represented much less, collapsed the entire
global banking system.

Technologically, there are too few people holding
the knowledge to systems that are now considered vital.
The same can be said of the monetary systems—for
example, the Fed insists on black box operations in
conducting monetary matters--and crude oil, from which
we get everything from fertilizer to Tupperware to space
shuttles: the extent to which we are leveraged via oil is
incalculable."

We tend to think of crude oil as the feedstock for gasoline and jet
fuel, but it's also the feedstock for agriculture (fertilizers and transport),
plastics (a significant percentage of industrial products) and ultimately
everything else via transport. A recent report from British Petroleum
(Statistical Review of World Energy, June 2011) noted that renewable
energy sources accounted for a grand total of 1.8% of global energy
consumption, and most of this is from burning biomass (wood, etc.) and
hydropower. Less than 0.5% of the world's energy is supplied by wind,
tide, wave, solar and geothermal sources.

Conventional economists assure us that oil accounts for a smaller
percentage of the U.S. economy that it did in the 1970s; but does that
mean that the economy is any less vulnerable to supply disruptions? The
concept of leverage helps us understand how removing $650 billion in
crude oil from the U.S. economy (18 million barrels a day X 365 days =
6.5 billion barrels X $100 per barrel = $650 billion) is not just a simple
subtraction of 4.5% of total GDP ($14.7 trillion): an absence of oil would
trigger the implosion of the entire U.S. economy.

That's leverage. Conventional economists dismissed the idea that
U.S. housing was a highly leveraged sand pile. But the leverage piled on
leverage was self-evident: the consumer borrowing that fueled much of
the decade's growth in spending was leveraged off the housing bubble,

which also leveraged rising demand for lumber, granite countertops, high-end refrigerators, etc., as well as a stupendous mountain of derivatives, credit default swaps, mortgage-backed securities and other financial instruments which then leveraged up Wall Street's profits and valuations.

The entire sand pile collapsed once its riskiest grains--the designed-to-default subprime option-ARMs and no-document liar loans--succumbed to gravity.

A machine is only as reliable as its weakest part. When that part fails, the machine grinds to a halt. The U.S. financial system is constructed of defective parts, each weaker than the next.

As analyst Janet Tavakoli has detailed, fraud is now the business model of the U.S. financial system. Embezzlement, collusion, misrepresentation of risk, shadow banking and opaque intervention by the Federal Reserve and Federal agencies are not isolated incidents, they are the very fabric of our entire financial system, a system whose primary goal is to conjure illusions of temporary wealth. A corrupt system soon corrupts the good people within, and thus we find financial markets, accounting and institutions that exhibit the classic signs of what we might call the banality of financial evil: fraud, misrepresenting risk, propaganda and manipulation are now just "day jobs," unquestioned by those tasked with their continuation.

This isn't a judgment, it's simply reporting. The business model of financial fraud, misinformation and manipulation renders investing fundamentally treacherous for small investors. Markets held aloft by intervention and propaganda have a nasty way of breaking down violently, and when information has been massaged to serve specific political agendas, then investment decisions based on that information will prove disastrously misguided.

The U.S. economy has long been dependent on consumer spending. For a variety of structural reasons beyond the scope of this book, household income has stagnated since the early 1970s, and it declined significantly in real (adjusted for inflation) terms between 2000 and 2010.

How can consumer spending keep rising when consumers' incomes are flat or falling? As noted above, the answer has been to fill the widening gap between income and consumption with borrowed money.

There are two ways to accomplish this: lower interest rates to near-zero, so consumers can borrow more money with the same amount of income, and secondly, increase credit and loosen the guidelines so more people can borrow more money.

This low-interest rate, easy-money environment fueled the great housing bubble between 2001 and 2007. As their primary asset kept rising in value, households found that they could extract huge sums via home equity lines of credit and refinancing mortgages.

Trillions of dollars were extracted from the dramatic rise in housing values, and this borrowed money filled the gap between stagnant incomes and rising costs for healthcare, education and property taxes, to name but a few essentials whose costs far outpaced low official inflation.

These increasingly burdensome expenses rose much faster than income for several structural reasons: the cost basis of the U.S. economy was no longer constrained by competition or limits on Federal debt.

The basic dynamic is this: when money is "free," costs rise. If you had to explain why healthcare in the U.S. consumes 17% of our nation's GDP while other developed nations provide universal care for half that cost per capita (8% of their GDP), the answer boils down to "there's an unlimited amount of free money in the U.S. for healthcare." There are no real limits on Medicaid or Medicare spending, or on healthcare insurance.

In other words, the Federal government (what I term the Central State) has granted quasi-monopolies to healthcare and insurance cartels and unaccountable State fiefdoms.

Baumol's Disease describes the rising costs of sectors whose productivity gains lag behind more productive sectors. Thus education costs more even as manufactured goods fall in price, as labor-intensive education doesn't lend itself to leaps in mechanized productivity.

But Baumol's Disease doesn't explain why fighter aircraft now cost $300 million each when the "best of the best" five years ago cost $56 million, or how Medicare has leaped from $52 billion a year to over $600 billion a year in a decade. Nor does it explain why property taxes have risen 60% above inflation in the past 10 years.

What does explain these gigantic increases is quasi-monopoly powers granted to cartels and unaccountable State fiefdoms. With the public unable to opt out of government, then government expands and passes the costs onto the taxpayers.

These high fixed costs feed into each other in positive feedback loops. The skyrocketing cost of providing full healthcare insurance raises the cost of public education, as most of the expenses of education are for labor. Government raises taxes and fees to pay for its higher healthcare costs, burdening the economy with higher costs that provides no additional value. As earnings remain flat and costs keep rising, the net result is household disposable income declines.

In a consumption-dependent economy, that decline causes the economy to shrink.

"The ratchet effect" describes the ease with which organizations and bureaucracies add staff and expenses and the difficulty of cutting expenses once revenue declines. Expenses ratchet up but they do not ratchet down, as embedded constituencies devote all their resources to self-preservation.

When the economy can no longer support its vast web of high-cost structures, then borrowing fills the gap between rising expenses and stagnant incomes. But eventually the cost of servicing this ever-increasing debt exceeds the carrying capacity of the economy, and the Status Quo tips into insolvency.

The vast speculative rewards for leveraged debt, i.e. "financialization," created perverse incentives that completely distorted the economy. The key feature of financialization is that the outsized profits come not from producing goods and services but from misrepresenting risk and gaming regulations intended to limit risk-taking.

Financialization inevitably leads to economy-wide misallocation of capital and massively mispriced risk.

Banks made money not from making prudent loans but from originating $30 of risk-laden loans from $1 in capital, and Wall Street reaped billions by packaging high-risk mortgages as "low-risk" investments. As we have seen, leveraging enables stupendous profits to flow to those with the best access to credit at low rates of interest, while government guarantees enabled Wall Street to ignore (i.e. misprice) risk.

As cheap, abundant credit washed into the economy, several things happened:

1) Speculative "hot money" seeking a higher return than the low yields offered on savings flowed into increasingly marginal investments. In a real-world example, investors built subdivisions in the middle of nowhere and then added a huge shopping mall to serve all the phantom shoppers who were expected to fill the new homes. But there was no real demand for the houses in the middle of nowhere—they were built to feed speculative demand. Once the speculative bubble popped, the builders and investors were exposed as insolvent.

2) Marginal borrowers, those who didn't have the assets or income to justify additional credit, were given abundant borrowing power. This increased the systemic risk as those marginal borrowers were extremely vulnerable to default once the asset bubble popped.

It turns out the market isn't very good at pricing the risk created by rising levels of leverage and credit-fueled speculation, especially when those risks are misrepresented with "ultra-safe" AAA ratings. Complex financial instruments such as credit-default swaps and other derivatives provided a "hiding in plain sight" screen of deliberate obfuscation that made risk assessment impossible.

With these incentives in place, everyone over-borrows and over-speculates in unproductive financial gambling until the asset bubble "unexpectedly" deflates.

The housing bubble offered the ambitious citizen a rare opportunity to leverage up just like Wall Street. Anyone with sufficient chutzpah could buy a number of houses with no-document, option-adjustable rate loans at super-low interest, hold the homes for a few months and then flip them for outsized profits.

A few thousand dollars in closing and carrying costs could be leveraged into tens of thousands of dollars in profits which could then be pyramided into more leverage.

The small-scale gamblers soon discovered a key difference between their own reckless speculation and Wall Street's: the over-leveraged real estate speculator was chided as irresponsible when his mini-empire of debt collapsed, while Wall Street was "saved" by trillions of dollars in Federal cash, backstops and guarantees.

In effect, as private borrowing and spending contracted, the Federal government has filled the gap by borrowing $1.5 trillion a year in deficit spending. Federally guaranteed or owned mortgage, consumer and student-loan debt now far surpasses private mortgage and consumer debt. The Central State is now propping up borrowing and spending on a vast scale (11% of the nation's GDP every year) that is unprecedented in our history, and there is no evidence that private borrowing and spending are recovering. Should Federal borrowing and spending decline, the illusion of "growth" will vanish.

With incomes declining, housing assets imploding and banks suddenly risk-averse, consumers can no longer borrow to fill the gap between their income and their consumption. In response to the end of credit-based consumer spending, the Federal government borrowed and spent $6 trillion over the past four years to fill the gaping hole in private consumption. This effectively doubled the Federal debt, a rate of increase that will quickly push public debt to crushing levels.

Two bad things happen in this nationwide financial overshoot. One is that all that new debt must be serviced, i.e. the interest and some modest attempt to pay down principal must be paid. In the virtuous up-cycle, rising profits and asset prices make borrowing more to pay the interest easy.

But once the debt cycle breaks, then assets and incomes both plummet, leaving borrowers unable to borrow more to pay the interest on their current debt.

As income streams and assets both decline, the interest payments, once lighter than air, soon drag the borrowers under water.

If we assemble all these systemic dynamics—the increasing dependence on fraud, leverage, super-low interest rates, expanding credit and Federal borrowing, the "ratchet effect" high cost-structure of the economy and the end of the postwar consumer-driven expansion— then we get a true understanding of the intrinsic instabilities and limits of both the U.S. economy and the global economy.

The rising centralization of financial power greatly increases the vulnerability of the system to disruption, as we have all become increasingly dependent on highly centralized financial systems. Transparency has been lost as much of this centralized power now resides in shadow institutions whose workings are opaque and largely outside the oversight of formal institutions; accountability has eroded to near-zero.

One way to understand the vulnerability of the system is to view it as a financial "ecosystem." A healthy financial ecosystem's many interactions establish a dynamic harmony of ebbs and flows within a stable, highly diverse framework. All ecosystems are inter-dependent, decentralized, and self-organizing—the very opposite of a centralized, top-down economy propped up by massive Central Bank intervention.

The strength of a stable financial ecosystem lies in the adaptability of the myriad enterprises in its many micro-climates and in the diversity of its many participants. Diversity and adaptability go together; each is a feature of the other.

The Federal Reserve has created an unstable monoculture of an economy, one dominated by a few large financial-sector parasites that can only survive if credit is always expanding and financialization continues to reap vast profits. But since it is impossible for these conditions to continue, the parasitic banks are vulnerable to collapse. And since Central Bank centralization has left the system a monoculture that is dependent on the "too big to fail" banks, when they implode the entire financial ecosystem is fatally disrupted.

In effect, the Federal Reserve has taken the risk from these failed institutions and spread it throughout the entire financial ecosystem. What should have triggered a "die off" of one predatory species--the "too big to fail" mortgage/commercial banks and the Wall Street investment banks-- was redistributed to all other participants.

In other words, the risk to the entire ecosystem has been raised in order to preserve the "too big to fail" predators. In redistributing the predators' monumental losses and the equally monumental risks of price discovery inherent in their undeclared losses, the Federal Reserve has greatly increased the vulnerability of the entire financial ecosystem.

In summary: in insulating participants from risk, fact-finding, and fluctuations (volatility), you make price discovery and thus stability impossible. Any stability that is forced on a system via intervention and purposeful obfuscation is merely a veneer of apparent stability waiting for an excuse to shatter.

Sadly, the incentives for productive investment and complying with the rule of law have declined while the incentives to "game the system," obfuscate, misrepresent and "beat the system" via lobbying, creative accounting and contributions to elected officials have dramatically increased. This cultural acceptance of cheating, political bribes and financial fraud as normal or even necessary for advancement has created a self-reinforcing cycle of ever-deepening dishonesty, masked by ginned-up statistics, propaganda and "hiding in plain sight" complexity.

There are six other critical issues that are compounding systemic risk.

1) As economist Hernando DeSoto has observed, the U.S. financial system has destroyed the infrastructure of facts which enabled accurate risk assessment. It is now difficult to say what entity has clear title to a house and the land beneath it in the U.S.; the entire system of land and mortgage recording has been overthrown to enable the bundling and tranching of home mortgages into mortgage-backed securities, a process

which was made much more profitable by jettisoning the cumbersome county-based system of land title and mortgage recording.

Nobody knows the full extent of the derivatives floating around the global financial system, or exactly what entities are exposed to counterparty loss; the "financial reforms" are riddled with so many loopholes and exemptions that they are nothing but flimsy facades designed to foster an illusion of reform.

A system in which public record facts and transparent documentation of exposure to risk are seen as inconvenient impediments to profit is a thoroughly corrupt and doomed system.

This erosion of the infrastructure of facts that is the foundation of the financial ecosystem has infected the entire U.S. legal system, which has slipped from "rule of law" to "purchase of favors, exemptions, subsidies and loopholes" via intense lobbying and large campaign contributions to elected officials. The legally indefensible machinations of the "too big to fail" banks to hide their liabilities and hurry through dubious foreclosures nonetheless find ready defenders in government and in wolf packs of "hired-gun" attorneys.

2) Many sober, experienced public figures are deeply concerned about the steady erosion of American citizens' civil liberties and legal rights, as stories about unlawful entry by law enforcement, extortion by local authorities and confiscation of private property become commonplace. An increasing number of citizens believe the U.S. is slipping from a rule-of-law State to a "banana republic" kleptocracy with two sets of laws: one for the wealthy and political Elites, and another for the commoners.

3) As I have often noted on my weblog, we are entering what author Jeremy Rifkin identified as "the end of work," an era in which the conventional sources of lifetime employment and retirement funding (i.e. the FIRE sector of finance, real estate and insurance, Corporate America and the Central State) are declining. Previous industrial sources of stable income have been disrupted by globalization and advances in robotics and software, a fate shared by low-productivity, high-cost service

sectors disrupted by the Internet. These realities are reflected in the stagnation of household income since 1970 that I have mentioned previously.

The net result of "the end of work" is that individuals, households and communities will have to foster more entrepreneurial, localized small businesses, and encourage informal work of the sort which sustains millions of people in developing economies. Incomes, just like other features of the economy, will become more volatile and less predictable, and retirement incomes will be disrupted or lost to creative destruction.

The adaptive solutions I present include diversification of income and what I term "hybrid work." I will discuss these issues later in the book.

The bottom line is that stable income in an unstable economy will no longer be a "sure thing," regardless of what promises have been issued by centralized authorities.

4) Four long-term trends are converging in the years ahead: resource depletion (a.k.a. the end of cheap oil, etc.), the four-generation cycle of dramatic social and economic change outlined in the book *The Fourth Turning*, the Kondratieff cycle of credit expansion and contraction/renunciation, and the long-wave increase in prices of essentials described in historian David Hackett Fischer's book, *The Great Wave: Price Revolutions and the Rhythm of History*.

In *The Fourth Turning*, authors William Strauss and Neil Howe posit a four-generation cycle that culminates in an epochal crisis every 80 years. This remarkable claim is supported by the pivotal dates in American history:

1781: Revolutionary War, independence of the United States
1861: American Civil War
1941: The Depression and beginning of World War II

If we extend the cycle, we can guess that 2021 might herald the "Grand Convergence" of the many unsustainable trends and cycles described in Chapter Two.

Many analysts have posited business cycles of varying lengths, for example, the original Kondratieff Cycle was reckoned at 26 years—26 years to a peak of credit and 26 years of decline to the trough.

In my view, a two-generation or 40-year cycle—half of a Strauss-Howe cycle--seems to align remarkably closely with the past century's financial peaks. Peaks of credit expansion and economic activity occurred around 1890, 1929 and 1969, and in each case these peaks were followed by a decade or more of stagnation, financial panic and credit renunciation. If we extend this cycle 40 years, it aligns rather neatly with the 2007-8 global top in growth, a peak reflected in oil prices. That suggests the following decade will be similarly troubled.

5) Systems analyst Cesare Marchetti in his 1996 paper, *Looking Forward - Looking Backward*, found that a vast spectrum of natural, social and economic activity tracked an S-curve, a statistical model that traces a line that looks like a flattened S: a period of slow, gradual increase followed by a steep rise, which then tops out. After the S-curve phase, activity declines.

Everything from the spread of plague to adoption of new technology fits this same model of gradual introduction, fast growth and eventual exhaustion. Though humans like to think of ourselves as free beings making conscious decisions, when our activity is tracked over a long period of time then it turns out our social and economic activities follow patterns that are very similar to those of non-conscious biological systems.

From the systems-analysis point of view, Peak Oil is not debatable, nor is it substantially influenced by new discoveries or reduced consumption; the timeline of growth, topping out and decline is statistically predictable.

A great many such foundations of developed-world economies are in the topping out or decline phase, including oil and credit as an engine of growth. As it now stands, each additional dollar of debt is generating less than a dollar of measurable growth. No policy tweak or adjustment of interest rate can change this fundamental characteristic of trends that have completed their cycle and are now in decline/depletion/diminishing return.

6) The Grand Convergence of these trends with the factors listed in Chapter One--technologically driven creative destruction not just of industries but of centralization everywhere, an accelerating pace of change, the grand failure of conventional economics and the simultaneous emergence of conflicting forces such as deflation and inflation—will create unprecedentedly complex and unpredictable dynamics. The sheer number, scale and speed of these interacting forces make it impossible to predict a neat and tidy outcome.

Indeed, questions that made sense in the old order, such as "will we have inflation or deflation?," or "How long will I have to work to build a retirement nest egg?" no longer make sense in this fluid, rapidly evolving vortex of destruction and adaptation.

Any one of these factors is sufficient to fatally disrupt the Status Quo, but all are converging in the same decade. Arguing about the impact of any one of these is like arguing about which of the six arrows embedded in the chest of the Status Quo is doing the most damage: it is irrelevant and a waste of time and energy.

Everyone whose lucrative livelihood depends on this system of institutionalized avoidance of fact and misrepresentation of risk has enormous incentives to protect it from real reform, and to champion its "health" and permanence. This devil's bargain of self-serving blindness feeds the financial system, as those who have gained the substantial compensation packages, a measure of workplace autonomy and the job security of insiders acquiesce to the exploitation of the bottom 95% by the top 5%--an exclusive club that they aspired to join and are willing to defend against all threats.

In doing so, they have betrayed both free enterprise and democracy.

This systemic overshoot has set in motion a destabilizing political momentum as well. The crumbling of the credit-bubble economy has mortally wounded the middle class, and this has created an insolvable problem for the Power Elites. In extending the credit-bubble economy-- that is, "wealth" is created via exponential expansion of debt--to housing, the Power Elites undermined the multigenerational bedrock of middle class wealth.

With housing equity stripped away, the erosion of middle class income and non-housing wealth has now been exposed.

The Power Elites' other wealth accumulation technique, globalization, has also gutted the middle class below the top 10% technocracy, and decimated the working class that had aspirations of joining the middle class, i.e. the lower middle class. Global Corporate America has decoupled from the American middle class; its interests are now international rather than domestic.

The Power Elites' response--borrow and squander trillions to prop up the engine of their own wealth, the banks, borrow trillions from future taxpayers to maintain the current Status Quo, and devalue the U.S. dollar--have all failed to reinflate housing or middle class incomes. Rather, these actions only succeeded in enriching the Cartel Corporatocracy and the top 10% who own the majority of stocks.

In destabilizing middle class wealth, the Power Elites have destabilized middle class political support for the Status Quo. Without that support, the Status Quo is living on borrowed time. The Status Quo's only "solution," to borrow trillions of dollars to prop up government spending and boost the speculative value of risk assets, is incapable of restoring middle class employment and wealth. Perversely, this stupendous Federal borrowing will only increase the tax burden on the middle class, further reducing their wealth.

At some point, the middle class will recognize the Status Quo as a parasitic burden, and remove their support. As author Thomas Homer-Dixon explained in *The Upside of Down*, this triggers the collapse of the Status Quo.

If you are like most investors, your instinct will be to reject this vast body of evidence because it means all the assumptions you're basing your decisions on are invalid, and this revolution in awareness is deeply unsettling. After all, what if I'm wrong and GDP growth continues merrily along for another ten years? This book will still have abundant value because it focuses on risk management and increasing your purchasing power—critical values regardless of what market or era you are navigating.

Prudent risk management requires us to ask precisely these kinds of anxiety-producing questions: what if the next 20 years have nothing in common with the past 20 years?

If we follow Harun's commentary to its logical end-state, then we have to conclude that the next 20 years cannot possibly be like the previous 20 years. We would also have to conclude that events that are currently considered "impossible" will not just become possible but increasingly likely.

Before deciding what is "impossible," we might recall that the bankruptcies of Enron, General Motors, Bear Stearns and Lehman Brothers were all considered "impossible" before their demise, and the global financial crisis of October 2008 was likewise "impossible" and entirely "unexpected" by conventional economists and advisors.

As Nassim Taleb of "black swan" fame has explained, it is misleading to say the last few grains of sand, for example, subprime mortgages in the housing bubble, are responsible for the entire sand pile collapsing: the masking of risk was systemic, and thus the sand pile was doomed to collapse regardless of the nature of the final few grains of sand.

Similarly, it won't really matter what the final trillion dollars of Federal debt was borrowed for; the default/collapse of the government debt pile is inevitable.

In betting the farm, so to speak, to prop up a façade of financial stability, the Federal Reserve and the Federal government have doomed the entire system to collapse. Taleb explained why in the June 2011 issue of *Foreign Affairs*: "Complex systems that have artificially suppressed volatility become extremely fragile, while at the same time exhibiting no visible risks." That describes the global economy in 2007, just before the financial meltdown of 2008 "surprised" conventional economists and Wall Street apologists.

As Taleb has explained, the very act of suppressing fluctuations renders systems extremely prone to large-scale disruptions that are viewed as low-probability events, the infamous "black swans." The key to understanding this rising likelihood of supposedly improbable disruptions is to understand the difference between linear and complex systems. Linear systems lend themselves to causal chains (A causes B which causes C) or probability (the odds of drawing two aces in a game of Blackjack) that can be calibrated with a high degree of accuracy.

Complex systems such as financial markets exhibit fractal or chaotic characteristics that lead to an unpredictability that is prone to disruption by seemingly small events. When volatility and risk (in political terms, dissent) are suppressed by central authorities, the variations that inform an open market ("variation is information") are lost.

The misrepresentation (and thus the mispricing) of risk and the suppression of volatility by Wall Street is a defect not of individuals or specific institutions but of the entire system, including the Federal Reserve, the Treasury and the regulatory "alphabet soup" agencies (SEC, FDIC, etc.).

The misguided attempts to engineer a false stability by suppressing volatility have created an intrinsically fragile system that is doomed to crises of ever greater dimension even as the periods of calm between crises shrink from years to months. Recall that risk is like water in a closed system: it can never be squeezed into nothingness. The more pressure that builds up, the more inevitable it is that the risk will burst out in some part of the financial system that was viewed as "safe" and "stable," for example, home mortgages.

This is how financial events that are widely viewed by conventional economists and government officials as "impossible" can occur with increasing frequency.

One model for this type of apparent stability that is disrupted by unpredictable spikes of volatility is stick/slip destabilization. In "sticky" systems—for example, those with major forces creating credit and regulations to maintain the Status Quo—pressure builds up within the system that is invisible to those looking at an apparently stable surface. But at some impossible-to-predict moment, the built-up pressure within completely disrupts the system, and it "slips" into a new and unpredictable configuration.

Here is a partial list of events deemed "impossible" now that I consider probable within the next ten years:
The financial markets will be restricted or closed for a time due to a financial or national "emergency."

1) Currency crises will destabilize foreign exchange.

2) Shortages in energy and/or food will trigger rationing.

3) Trading in precious metals, foreign exchange, oil and other commodities will be restricted.

4) Capital controls will limit the amount of capital that can be taken out of the country.

5) Financial contracts, trades and swaps will be negated by Force Majeure.

6) Some financial markets will shut down for lack of interest/participation.

7) The majority of asset classes will see staggering declines in real value, i.e. purchasing power, while others will leap to heights beyond current conception.

8) The government (Federal, state and local) will renege on its entitlement promises and bonds.

9) Asset prices will undergo unprecedented swings in valuation over increasingly shorter periods of time.

In sum: the rules of the investment/speculation "game" will be changed without warning as authorities attempt to stabilize an increasingly chaotic financial system. Their attempts to force a superficial stability will only make the next round of instability more severe and less controllable.

Perhaps none of these events will occur, or perhaps all will come to pass. No one knows the future. But to discount the probabilities of "unexpected" stick/slip destabilizations is to indulge in a potentially dangerous complacency.

The Grand Partnership of the Central State and the Financial

Plutocracy (parasitic globalized cartel crony-Capitalism writ large) has suppressed this natural implosion of speculative debt by printing and distributing trillions of dollars in "free" money so over-indebted borrowers and speculators can continue to "extend and pretend," that is, continue the illusion that they are solvent.

As a special bonus to these financial Power Elites, this limitless pool of "free money" enabled them to ramp up their favorite pastime, leveraged financial speculations based on fraud, collusion and misrepresentation of risk. As any profits will be theirs to keep while any losses will be backstopped by the Central State and its taxpayers, it's a return to the risk-free days at the races for the financial Oligarchy.

But massive doses of free money unleash two destructive forces on the economy: as the free money flows into speculative bets on tangible resources, it reinflates asset bubbles and fuels rising costs.

As a result, the system is now facing the same old problems--asset bubbles held aloft by "free money," massive government intervention, systemic financial fraud--and a new problem: price inflation for the resources that sustain the real economy.

The Central State/Financial Elites are thus faced with an impossible choice: if they let the speculative free money flow, then their populations become impoverished as the prices of tangible goods such as food and energy skyrocket. Recall that the masses aren't provided with billions of dollars at zero interest; that privilege is reserved for the financial Elites who fund the campaigns of the Central State's political class.

The Classical Capitalist answer to this vast financial overshoot is simple: once the unlimited free money and moral hazard guarantees stop, interest rates will rise as risk is repriced and the market "discovers" the cost of borrowing scarce capital (savings). Once interest rates rise, then the ballooning debt can no longer be serviced. Borrowers big and small go bankrupt, their assets are sold at auction on the open market, and their unpaid debts are absorbed as losses by their creditors.

This renunciation of debt triggers a domino effect as credit becomes increasingly expensive and other overleveraged borrowers and insolvent creditors are toppled into bankruptcy.

In other words, the Status Quo is now addicted to unlimited flows of free credit issued by central banks. If the flow continues, then inflation will destabilize it; if it's cut off, then rising interest payments will destabilize it. No matter what policy path is taken, the result is the same: destabilization.

This is why a systemic financial meltdown is now inevitable.

Nobody knows how this devolution will play out, but we do know that those who are open to the possibility will do better than those who discount or dismiss the inevitable reckoning as "impossible."

3 | An (Anachronistic) Observer's Perspective

Conventional economists and stock market analysts fall into one of two camps: those who expect a return to permanently rising prosperity (as measured by Gross Domestic Product, GDP), and those who expect a "muddle through" or "sideways trading market" dominated by a stagflation similar to the 1970s, followed by a return to permanently rising prosperity.

Given that the next 20 years will necessarily be different from the previous 20 years and unprecedented in human history, then expecting a sideways trading market for years to come is to ignore all the factors outlined in the previous chapters. In other words, muddle-through and sideways markets are as low probability futures as a global Bull market because they're both based on the premise that the Status Quo is not only sustainable but is essentially unthreatened by systemic instabilities.

We've had a muddle-through market recently thanks to unprecedented Central State and central bank intervention, but the limits of those policies are already squeezing the real economy. We've had anything but a sideways market since 2008, as stocks tumbled and then doubled, and the lifeblood of the global industrial economy—oil--gyrated wildly, plummeting from $140 per barrel in 2008 to $32 in 2009 and then surging to over $100 per barrel in 2011, all in the space of three years.

We are in an era not of sideways meandering but of enduring instability and volatility, and we will see the rules changing before our eyes as those at the top of the heap seek to prop up an unsustainable and overextended Status Quo by whatever means are at hand. Investing rules will vanish into thin air, statistics will veer further into disinformation, and facsimiles of reform will be paraded as "fixes."

On the other side of the ledger are those who anticipate the unraveling of unsustainable systems, i.e. "doom and gloomers," many of whom foresee a collapse of the industrial economy and terminal social disorder. For many in this camp, the key investments are bullion and bullets. (For those who don't grasp the relationship between the two, I will paraphrase a common survivalist meme: "You have stockpiled gold, I have stockpiled lead, and I'll be along shortly to collect your gold.")

In my view, gold offers a unique hedge against instability, a topic I will cover later. If this makes me a "doom and gloomer," then so be it. I believe in hedging against possibilities which could have catastrophic consequences. This seems mere prudence. As for those who reckon the probabilities of a global financial meltdown are low: low-probability events occur with remarkable regularity. Hedging is less about probabilities (often wrong) and more about possibilities (often correct).

Having written a book titled *Survival+: Structuring Prosperity for Yourself and the Nation*, it's clear that I am in the "don't expect the Status Quo to endure" side—but not in the terminal social disorder camp. I believe that the key human traits of community, innovation and adaptability will mitigate the disorder caused by the messy devolution of the cheap energy/centralized State/debt-dependent Status Quo.

In other words, there are things we can do to retain our rights, our property and our prosperity, but they don't involve putting your faith in the promises and propaganda of the Status Quo.

I'm going to be very blunt here about the key issues which any book on investing must address, either explicitly or implicitly. You may not like my approach, or you may find it too "obvious" to be useful. I suspect that the more experience you have in actual trading and entrepreneurial enterprise, and in the contemplation and pursuit of happiness, the more value you will find here.

Let's start with a disclosure of self-interest: I have nothing to sell you except this book, which is exceedingly modest in cost compared to 2% annual management fees or several hundred dollars a year in newsletter subscription fees. I do not manage others' money nor do I have any interest in doing so. A primary principle of this book is the only person qualified to manage your capital is you.

I do not make my living in the investment industry; I am an observer who makes my living from writing and from work in the tangible, real world. If you want exciting tales from inside hedge funds, you won't find them here.

Rather than follow the conventional strictures of investment books— i.e. focus narrowly on technical analysis and financial strategies--this book has a much more expansive purpose and vision.

What I am offering is a wide-ranging perspective on our era and on the process of change that we experience as instability, unpredictability and volatility. Frankly, I don't see how anyone can avoid catastrophic losses of capital, much less become prosperous, if they ignore the unprecedented nature of this era.

While conventional investment is studiously apolitical, in my view all investment decisions are inescapably political. If you give your capital to Wall Street to play with and borrow money from "too big to fail" banks, then you are "voting" for a deeply corrupt, parasitical and doomed system. Our participation is what gives the Status Quo power over our economy and governance. There is no way to escape this choice between participation/complicity and non-participation, or the moral and financial consequences of complicity. If we participate, then we are complicit in the subversion of democracy that is the very heart of the centralized, financialized Status Quo.

In the conventional investment perspective, amassing concentrations of wealth is presumed to be the key goal of work and life. The unsaid assumption is that concentrations of wealth will magically make us secure and happy. Yet studies of human happiness find no such causal link. Rather, the things which create happiness are only marginally connected to money or wealth: health, family enduring friendships, purpose, productive engagement in the real world, and other forms of social capital.

The conventional investment advisor selling their service harrumphs that wealth is the grease to all these forms of happiness, but that is both self-serving and untrue: money's role in happiness and fulfillment is modest. The key question here is *cui bono*—to whose benefit? Our belief in the magical power of money to make us happy and secure enables the conventional investment industry's lucrative fees.

Furthermore, in an era of unprecedented creative destruction and instability, to make the implicit promise that wealth can be concentrated and preserved for decades to come is itself a self-serving and misleading illusion. Rather than promise security, counting on a concentration of wealth for security is akin to relying on a monoculture crop: rather than being a source of security, it is instead a source of systemic risk and insecurity. It's the decentralized, resilient ecosystem which offers security, not the centralized, concentrated monoculture.

As a result, this book is deeply and fundamentally subversive to the Status Quo and the conventional investment industry. I concede this but prefer the less inflammatory word "anachronistic" to describe my perspective.

This book's perspective can be roughly distilled into these points:
1) In depending on financialization and debt for growth, we have handed the keys to the castle, so to speak, to the cartel banks and Wall Street. Their concentrated political power flows directly from our reliance on their leverage and legerdemain. Thus political control of the banks and Wall Street is impossible unless we stop depending on their centralized systems of financialization and debt.
2) Centralization, monopoly, corruption and misallocation of capital are like the fingers of one hand. If you have to corrupt 1,000 people peppered over a decentralized economy, then the gain from each is tiny—hardly worth the effort. Corrupting a handful of top officials with centralized authority, on the other hand, is a low-cost way of insuring huge gains.
3) Disruptive technologies undermine centralized monopolies, and so they also disrupt political power. The printing press dismantled the Catholic Church's monopoly on biblical knowledge, for example, and that eventually disrupted the church's centralized political power.
4) By undermining the competitive advantages of centralization, decentralized digital technologies will eventually disrupt all centralized institutions, including finance, healthcare, education,

government and everything else considered "safe" from creative destruction.

5) The easy low-risk profits come from monopolies and cartels. This is the advantage of centralization, and why Power Elites recruit governments to protect their cartels from competition and why governments secure monopolies for themselves. The irresistible destroyer of cartels is new technology that is so much more efficient that clinging to the past source of their power dooms both cartels and parasitic governments.

Risk and return are bound together; there is no return without risk. To believe that risk can be compressed into nothingness is to put your faith in a dangerous illusion. Risk is part of the landscape, and doing nothing can be just as risky as taking action.

1) There are no surefire techniques for identifying the "next big thing" technology and so risk is intrinsic to technological change.

2) The most productive model for understanding the economy and enterprise is the ecosystem.

3) Simplicity in production of value and diversity of supply sources are both advantageous. Diverse assets and sources of income create resilience. Dependence on one source of income or one asset creates high risk and extreme vulnerability.

4) The most productive model for individual investors is to view themselves and their household as an integrated, dynamic enterprise within a complex, dynamic financial ecosystem.

5) Those who become comfortable with uncertainty and unpredictability will be happier in an era of unprecedented change and volatility than those who cling to systems and ideologies undergoing creative destruction.

6) All investments are speculations.

7) All investments are profoundly political, and cannot be apolitical.

8) Of the three types of capital—financial, human and social—it is social capital which will become increasingly valuable as a source of security and well-being.

9) New technology-enabled models of decentralization and transparency are bypassing, and thus democratizing, corrupt concentrations of centralized financial and political power.

10) Money is a tool; don't invest your money in Wall Street's promises, invest it with an unblinking eye on systemic risk. Invest in your own life and in the lives of others.

I titled this book *Investing in Troubled Times* for three reasons beyond the premise that the Status Quo cannot possibly continue in its current course: one, creative destruction of the Status Quo will create asymmetric valuations which can be exploited by those who understand that centralization is no longer a productive model; two, the extraordinary unpredictability of troubled times offers equally extraordinary opportunities to create decentralized, resilient enterprises and communities; and three, "investing" covers not just financial instruments like stocks and bonds but a wide spectrum of other investments and hedges, including non-market investments such as building social capital and multiple sources of income.

Indeed, large-scale studies of happiness have found that social capital and trust, not financial wealth or benefits, are the foundations of happiness among populations around the globe. For individuals, the social capital provided by friends, family and colleagues and the human capital provided by skills and a purposeful life are the foundations of happiness.

In the U.S., our understanding of enterprise has been reduced to an obsession with "maximizing profit" and concentrating private financial wealth. Given that happiness has little causal connection to amassing concentrations of wealth or maximizing profits, then America's obsession with these goals is revealed as not just unhealthy and counter-productive but profoundly misguided. Stripping enterprise and life down to profits and concentrating wealth is actually a path to a deeply deranged state of poverty.

My perspective is that of a practical person. I am not a theoretical entrepreneur or trader; rather, I follow Emerson's dictum to "do the thing and you shall have the power." Everyone's situation is unique to them, and thus the mix of tools and strategies that fit their circumstance will be equally unique. This aligns with my view that the only person who is qualified to make investment decisions for you is you.

I am keenly aware that millions of people have little to no financial capital, and millions of others have much of their financial capital trapped in 401K and IRA retirement funds which often limit their investing options to a handful of funds. Advising them to invest their capital in a farm and a diesel generator is not entirely practical because much of their capital is tied up in restricted retirement accounts, and they must struggle to preserve the purchasing power of this capital until they can withdraw it.

While I am a proponent of tools, productive land, energy generation and water rights, I also recognize that the vast majority of jobs are located in urban and suburban zones, and so investing in real assets must address a spectrum of potential situations—including investing in local enterprises. Those with 401Ks and IRAs must live within the limitations of those structures, and so a multi-track investment strategy becomes an appropriate model. Investments can be made in a spectrum running from what I call centralized market investments, i.e. global markets, to decentralized investments made in local businesses, one's own skills, and income streams which are independent of the global markets.

One size definitely does not fit all, and my goal is to offer a banquet of options and analytic tools to help each person and household put their capital (money and time) to the most productive uses available to them. Diversity of income streams and assets creates resilience; dependence on one asset class or income creates vulnerability.

"Investing" is a misnomer: every investment is a speculation, unless it is an embezzlement based on insider trading and fraud, i.e. the standard Wall Street "investment." The only difference between various speculations is the length of time that is needed for the speculation to pay off. A high-frequency trading machine, i.e. a quant black box, is programmed to execute a trading algorithm with a timeline of a few moments: investing in a new oil well requires a timeline of years before a payoff is realized, but it too is a speculation.

Even "investments" such as going to college are ultimately speculations, as the future gains are unknown.

I prefer the word speculation, even though it has an unsavory connotation, because it also implies risk and uncertainty: every speculation is a gamble, and that aligns much more closely to reality in my view than the bland, safe-sounding "investment," which is misleading in its connotation of stability and low risk.

There is no such thing as low risk; there is only transparent risk, and masked or misrepresented risk.

As a convention, however, I will use the words "investment" and "investing," but always with the understanding that all investments are speculations—unless of course, the Central State has rigged the market in favor of a cartel crony-capitalist skimming scheme such as high-frequency trading.

Capitalism has been smeared by crony "capitalism" and cartel/monopoly "capitalism," both of which are the opposite of true open-market capitalism in that each purposefully eliminates competition and off-loads risk onto the taxpayer via Central State bailouts, subsidies and guarantees.

Open-market capitalism is the deployment of scarce capital in a transparently risky enterprise that the entrepreneur hopes will be productive. This classic form of capitalism is highly individualistic, as the decision to invest time and capital are left to individuals rather than cartels or the Central State. Unproductive assets soon lose value and are liquidated—"fail small, fail fast"--while productive assets create surplus income (profits) which attracts talent and additional capital. This dynamic creates employment and wealth, which can then be reinvested in new productive enterprises.

Capitalism is not a perfect system but rather a construct of imperfect human nature. Extreme concentrations of wealth easily convert into extremes of political power, and as a result a free people benefit from a decentralized, democratic balance-of-powers Central State which is empowered to limit extreme concentrations of privately held power, one of which is Monarchy and another is oligarchy, As is demonstrated daily, concentrated wealth subverts the Central State via capture of its machinery of governance and regulation. That is how we end up with crony "capitalism" and cartel/monopoly "capitalism" which are enabled and protected by an intrusive Central State. Banks and corporations have effectively bought the Central State via campaign contributions to elected officials and a revolving door between two sets of foxes assigned to guard the henhouse: Wall Street and the "too big to fail" banks, and the financial regulatory agencies in Washington.

In broad-brush, that is the unstable backdrop to all our investing options and decisions.

I believe the solutions are decentralization of political power and the freedom to form enterprises free of the corrupting influence of cartels and their partner in plunder and pillage, the Central State. I see dependence on the Central State, for "bread and circuses" or monopoly, as extremely debilitating for individuals, enterprises and the nation. The Central State has two key roles in civil society: to restrict and punish predation by individuals and Elites, and to limit the predation of its own Elites and bureaucracies.

These views do not necessarily fit neatly into prepackaged ideological "boxes."

I consider enterprise and innovation, both technological and social/behavioral, as the key components of diversity and adaptability, the two traits which are most valuable in rapidly evolving (or devolving) times. Thus investing capital and time in enterprises you control is a critical component of any diverse investment strategy.

I see the deeply intertwined forces of centralization and financialization as major systemic vulnerabilities which cannot be engineered away. The centralization and opacity of financial power renders these systems inherently unstable. The more we rely on centralized concentrations of financial power, the more vulnerable we are to disruptions in those systems.

The conventional money manager reckons that spreading assets over stocks, bonds and commodities in both global and domestic markets is a diversifying strategy that lowers risk. From my point of view, these are just facets of the same trade in an increasingly unstable global system, and thus they represent very little diversification in troubled times. As I noted earlier, the governments' propping up of assets introduces moral hazard on a grand scale; this is one reason why all global markets move as one trade.

The global markets in stocks, bonds and commodities have one potential value: as highly liquid hedges that can be bought and sold easily.

From my point of view, any long-term investment in these global markets might end up yielding a peculiarly unsatisfactory dividend, such as a notice of expropriation from a new junta, a default announcement, a notification of Force Majeure or perhaps a government-issued "new currency."

I also think anyone writing about investing and speculating has a duty to disclose their own track record. Simply put, I am either the world's worst trader, or in the running for that dubious title. My character and personality are perniciously opposite those of the naturally talented trader: I am impatient, impulsive, reckless, resistant to selling for a loss, a natural-born contrarian in a market which goes up most of the time, overly excitable when calmness is required, and a manic-depressive prone to wild swings of disillusion and confidence. If that wasn't bad enough, I also have a boundless appetite for risk, which feels like power instead of reckless stupidity.

Despite this perfection of destructive traits, I have made a handful of speculations that yielded 20-fold gains and turned a modest five-figure position into a seven-figure position. Thus I have the experience to study successful trades from the inside, as well as ample experience in recklessly wrongheaded speculations. In the late 1990s I worked in the San Francisco-based back office of a very savvy quantitative analyst,

Stewart Pillette. This experience helped me understand quantitative analysis and how fund managers—the firm's primary clients —ply their trade.

I try to practice what I preach. My primary assets are my skills, which cannot be lost, appropriated or stolen, my health, my family, friends, neighbors, readers and customers, and my willingness to evolve, diversify, adapt and learn.

In my 20s, we lived for a time in a plywood shack built with hand tools, without water or power, and were quite happy doing so. The measure of wealth, happiness and even prosperity is not necessarily financial, yet our culture and economy are structured as if that is the only metric of value in the universe. It isn't.

I have no idea what will happen in the future. But then neither does anyone else. We're all guessing. Probabilities are helpful, but they can foster a false sense of precision: low probability events seem to occur with surprising regularity, and high-probability events can suddenly become low-probability. Models and projections of recent trends are also helpful, but models are based on past patterns which might have little to no value if the future doesn't echo the recent past.

As William Byers of Concordia University has noted, reliance on quantification is inherently risky due to weaknesses intrinsic in all statistical models: 1) they filter out ambiguity, 2) the reduction to numbers reinforces a belief in linear comparisons and projections that ignore qualitative factors, and 3) any system that involves human behavior is necessarily self-referential.

Projections are especially prone to false precision. If one team in a basketball game scores a quick 8 points at the start while their opponents remain scoreless, then projecting that data to the end of the game would lead to an estimated score of 148 to 0.

All we can do is be alert and flexible, and be open to relative performance, asymmetric valuations and trend reversals.

I have often been an active trader in options and equities over the past 16 years. I now practice what my mentor Harun characterizes as "guerrilla investing:" hiding quietly in the jungle until a low-risk opportunity arises, emerging to make the trade and exit with the gains, and then fade back into the shadows, out of harm's way, until the next opportunity arises.

If the guerrilla metaphor strikes you as too martial, then a hunter-gatherer metaphor works just as well, if not better: the hunter-gatherer carefully studies the terrain and knows the watering holes and fecund fruit trees, and doesn't waste precious time and energy wandering around the wastelands looking for the occasional grub and root. The gatherer notes the habits and routes of predators and competitors, and avoids needlessly risky encounters with them. He or she waits patiently for the season to announce the ripening of the fruit, and only then does he or she make the trip out to the trees that others have missed or passed too early to harvest.

What I have to offer you is not advice or recommendations, but a perspective informed by my experience that seeks true diversification and the maximization of your skills and capital. Nobody knows what the future will bring, so the best that we can do is to be alert to risks and opportunities, stay focused on what nurtures happiness and and fulfillment, and be willing to adapt and evolve in our understanding and actions.

Given the essential role social and human capital have in happiness and security, it is unsurprising that this book devotes considerable time to those forms of capital. It should also be unsurprising that I take a somewhat detached view of the possibility that we are entering the equivalent of a black hole, in which current forms of financial wealth will be stripped away, revalued or transformed as we exit the event horizon into a new era.

Although nobody knows the future, I strongly suspect that financial engineering will not retain its current value. Rather, I expect it to lose all credibility long before then, along with Wall Street as it is currently configured.

From this point of view, the entire notion of "saving for retirement" within a global marketplace dominated by Wall Street, hedge funds, complicit government agencies and "too big to fail" banks is an artifact of the financially stable world that is rapidly receding in the rear view mirror.

We can safely assume that productive land and sources of energy, low-maintenance infrastructure, metals, fresh water, shelter, good governance, liberty, communities that maintain open markets for goods and services, and a spectrum of skills will retain value in any future short of a 100-mile diameter meteor striking the Earth.

The list does not include mutual funds, stocks, bonds, derivatives, or any paper money. The purchasing-power value of such financial instruments is based on trust, and if trust—what we might call the symbolic confidence we place in paper money as a claim on real goods-- has been stripped away by excesses, dishonesty, and abuses of power, then they may be valued quite differently, or even rendered worthless.

As the Federal Reserve of Chicago noted in a 1961 paper, *Modern Money Mechanics*: "What, then, makes these instruments - checks, paper money, and (base metal) coins - acceptable at face value in payment of all debts and for other monetary uses? Mainly, it is the confidence people have that they will be able to exchange such money for other financial assets and for real goods and services whenever they choose to do so."

If degradation of that confidence or the erosion of paper money's value via high inflation are distinct possibilities based on history, then we are duty-bound to question the deeply ingrained idea that setting aside today's income in symbolic claims on future goods and services makes sense.

Does it make sense to laboriously squirrel away $1 million earned by the sweat of decades of labor only to find that by the time I retire that sum will buy a used auto, or perhaps a single bag of groceries? What if the financial authorities, in response to the latest "financial crisis," reset the paper currency at a rate of 100 "old dollars" to one "new dollar," effectively wiping out 99% of the purchasing power of my retirement nest egg?

Put another way, what we're "saving up" when we accumulate paper money (or other paper like stocks and bonds) are claims on future goods and services. What is the durability of such claims? If we think through the consequences of the previous chapters, we have to conclude that expecting the cash in our retirement accounts to retain their current value a few decades hence is quite a long shot.

Oftwominds.com correspondent John Harper recently posed this question to me: If extreme concentrations of wealth are a primary cause of exploitation and financial instability in our economy, then why do we assume that aspiring to concentrate wealth is somehow a good thing?

Indeed, studies of lottery winners have found that quite often great wealth is a source of anxiety and unhappiness, and the winner of the wealth only finds equanimity and happiness after he has lost or spent the wealth. Having to protect their wealth from grifters, thieves, relatives, con-men and the authorities simply wasn't worth the benefits of concentrated wealth, which turned out to be much less than advertised.

While some misers have managed to stash secret fortunes beneath ragtag lives of deprivation, the average human being with a concentration of wealth—for example, a hoard of gold—is unable to convincingly evince abject poverty. Their concentration of wealth creates attractive targets for theft or confiscation by authorities desperate for funds to stave off the latest "financial crisis." As many of you know, the Federal government decided it prudent to confiscate privately held gold in 1933 (Executive Order 6102 permitted ownership of up to $100 in gold, roughly 5 troy ounces person, as well as collectible coins). Various other government measures achieve the same result: confiscation and/or destruction of private wealth.

As noted above, attempts to insulate wealth from risk have the pernicious consequence of removing fluctuations and volatility that are actually key sources of information ("variation is information"). Without accurate information and price discovery, then the system is headed for instability and collapse.

Referencing the previous discussion of financial ecosystems, a concentration of wealth is somewhat akin to a monoculture crop that is, by virtue of its dominance of the ecosystem, exceedingly vulnerable to fast-spreading crises and thus to collapse. Diversity, exposure to the information communicated by volatility, dissent, and other forms of continuous but low-amplitude instability ("fail fast, fail small, fail often"), and willingness to experience the gains and losses inherent to adaptations are the characteristics of successful ecosystems and organisms. These are also characteristics of stable financial systems and enterprises.

From this point of view, our capital and income can be understood as a financial ecosystem within a larger ecosystem, rather than as a series of discrete accounts such as "retirement," "housing," and so on. Rather than attempt to accumulate and set aside some systemically risky claims on future goods and services, i.e. retirement, or a nest egg of wealth that might or might not come through the coming transformation with the anticipated value, we might look at our life, work and finances as a complex enterprise which benefits from the same features found in resilient, resource-rich ecosystems: diversity of capital and income streams, openness to the signals provided by low-intensity volatility and dissent, and a preference for adaptation and experimentation.

I would like to stress once again that the critical risks to the Status Quo are intrinsic and structural, and the key features of increasingly unstable complex systems are volatility and unpredictability.

Many people obsess over specific questions, such as, "Will we have deflation or inflation?" with the idea that answering this question will enable them to hold onto their wealth or even create great wealth. Viewed from the perspective of an increasingly unstable complex system, the question is more distracting than useful.

If David Hackett Fischer's model of the history of price proves accurate, then the cost of essentials such as food and energy (as measured by the purchasing power of an hour of labor) will rise inexorably as the human population and financial system have both exceeded the carrying capacity of resources.

Meanwhile, discretionary assets such as pleasure yachts and vacation homes might drop significantly in price as more of the national income is diverted to buy essentials (what I call the FEW essentials: food, energy and water). Many would call this asset deflation. Both of these conditions could occur within the same timeframe.

Many people assume that intrinsically unstable systems will move in a straight line to collapse. A more realistic model is "punctuated equilibrium," a concept borrowed from evolutionary science, which suggests that periods of relative stability where the organism in question is well-adapted to the environment are punctuated by brief period of extreme stress and adaptation when the environment suddenly changes. If the organism adapts successfully to the challenges, then a new equilibrium is established.

Thus it is possible that paper money might appreciate against tangible goods for a time. Alternatively, periods of rapid inflation might trigger a centralized response which quells the inflation and accompanying social disorder and establishes a period of relative equilibrium that is eventually punctuated by some new crisis. The main point is that any equilibrium in a fundamentally unstable system will be impermanent.

If natural systems are any guide, we might expect the duration of equilibrium phases to become shorter while the amplitude of each subsequent crisis rises. We might also expect that the increasing amounts of energy required to stabilize the Status Quo will sap the entire system of wealth and resilience, and as a result each plateau of relative calm will be at a lower level of consumption than the previous equilibrium.

The key feature we need to focus on is not a narrow financial question such as deflation or inflation, but on the system's inherent instability and unpredictability. The challenge is not to correctly guess the trend that will carry forward without interruption for the next 10 or 20 years, a question rendered irrelevant by the system's intrinsic instability, but on assembling an enterprise—you and your household--that has the characteristics of successful ecosystems: a rich diversity of capital and income streams that effectively gathers the wealth of information provided by low-intensity, low-amplitude instability, dissent and volatility ("fail fast, fail small, fail often"). Such enterprises will foster resilience and adaptability and thus be prepared to avoid potentially fatal spikes of high-intensity instability ("black swans").

Every enterprise is a form of self-expression. If an enterprise operates not as self-expression but in obedience to an agenda or purpose borrowed or imposed from elsewhere, then the individuals involved will be unable to muster the enthusiasm and energy required to make the enterprise a success in a fast-changing, unpredictable environment.

In a very real way, we can either invest our time and energy in trying to stabilize an unstable Status Quo, a project doomed to failure, or we can invest our time and energy in enterprises that encourage experimentation, adaptation, low concentrations of risk and wealth (i.e. widely distributed risk and capital), a rich diversity of capital and income streams, and a recognition of the unique "wealth" that flows from social capital.

I term these alternatives to centralized, globalized, financialized markets "transparent voluntary parallel structures," as they exist side-by-side with the dominant centralized corporatocracy, and are transparent, as opposed to the purposefully opaque cartel capitalism/Central State Status Quo.

We each have a choice: we can decide to limit our participation in the Status Quo, and participate in parallel, decentralized, transparent self-organizing alternatives.

No honest exploration of investing in troubled times can avoid the profound consequences of our industrialized dependence on fossil fuels, especially oil. Renewable energy sources provided a meager 1.8% of the world's energy consumption in 2010, and most of this was generated by hydropower and biofuels (burning wood, which practically speaking isn't renewable over the short-term). Even if this number doubles every few years, it will still be a long time before renewable sources provide a meaningful percentage of energy consumption, which continues to rise.

Even if energy sources are adequate to meet demand, the cost of the energy will be much higher, as the "easy oil" is already gone. As more earnings are diverted to pay for energy, less income is available for the sort of discretionary consumption which residents of the developed world have assumed as their birthright. The vast majority of households will thus be less prosperous, as more of the household income will be spent on energy and everything dependent on energy, such as food, transport, etc.

This is the basis of predictions that the standard of living for most households will decline.

Unlike earnings and energy, trust and social and human capital are still abundant, and in some ways, unlimited. Since happiness results from social capital and trust, then we can conclude that beyond the bare necessities of life—food, shelter, community and clean water—the sources of human happiness are unlimited.

From my perspective, this logic suggests that obsessing over our declining standard of living as measured by GDP or consumption of goods and services is a meaningless exercise, since rising consumption has no causal connection to happiness or increasing social capital and trust.

The obsession with rising consumption is thus a political construct, fabricated by those who benefit from an obsession with consuming more goods and services.

Much of what I present as self-evident is so far out of the mainstream that it may be new to you. That of course is its value.

For that is the peculiarly fecund marriage of risk and innovation. From the conventional perspective, innovation is extremely risky, because there are no proven models of success or "safe" pathways to follow. But ironically, perhaps, these are the precise reasons why innovation is much lower risk than jumping into a market already crowded with other competitors. It is the seed that falls into the clearing still warm from the forest fire that is most likely to gain the sun and the nutrients needed to thrive, while the seeds that fall in the forest thick with other competing growth that faces the higher risks and lower probability of survival.

This is where the most radical tenet of this book comes into play, for what powers uniqueness and thus innovation is self-expression. Our understanding of enterprise and investment has been reduced to a single pathetic squawk, parroted endlessly by a servile financial media: maximize profit, maximize profit, brawk!

If we examine this monomania more closely, we find it is entangled in our national identity and in the distorted structure of our economy and culture.

A key tenet of American economic life is that "looking out for Number One" is the only way to get ahead in a Darwinian competition for scarce resources. This is ironic, given that it is looking out for numbers two through twenty, i.e. social capital, which actually underpins human happiness. So this tough-sounding value system of "looking out for Number One" is actually a model for vulnerability, unhappiness and impoverishment.

If you want to experience this sort of impoverishment, visit an "exclusive" gated community that bans everything but walking your dog along approved trails (there are no sidewalks) and "community events" in an ersatz "community center." You rarely see anyone about, and whatever interactions do occur are limited to rote greetings.

Though superficially "wealthy" as measured in consumption, this is only a wealth of isolation and loneliness.

Americans are especially keen to avoid being conned by marketing, as nobody wants to be viewed as a chump, so this aggressively cynical obsession with maximizing profit is presented as "I'm nobody's fool" strength.

This too is ironic, for an obsession with maximizing profit is the greatest con of all, as it plays right into Wall Street's churn-and-skim machine. Our participation in the "maximizing profit is all that matters" value system is what fuels Wall Street's billions of dollars in annual profits, which is then deployed to subvert democracy, backstop private cartel losses and eliminate competition.

Those expressing the "looking out for Number One, maximizing profit is all that counts" value system are not tough-minded, they're weak-minded chumps who have fallen for Wall Street's most basic con.

When it comes to making decisions for oneself, the single-minded obsession with "maximize profits" misses the point about competition and innovation. Everyone else is trying to "maximize profit," a crowded, sunless forest indeed, while you are intent on expressing yourself. In that sense, you have no competition, and the path is open before you.

4| Our Need for Inspiration and Hope

The human mind has an innate distaste for uncertainty and complexity: it likes certainty and simplicity above all else. This is why people quickly tire of learning, practice, open-mindedness and analysis, and why they happily latch onto a simplistic ideology that "explains" the world around them. Once they've chosen their basic explanatory framework, then they resist examining or questioning it.

People will make a decision simply to get rid of uncertainty. Once that uncertainty has been replaced with certainty, then humans cling to that certainty rather than suffer another bout of uncertainty. But the world is intrinsically uncertain, and so this desire for certainty leads to a disconnect between reality (uncertain) and our inner model of the world (certainty).

As noted above, it is the ability to gather low-amplitude information (instability, dissent and ambiguity) which enables successful adaptation in volatile, troubled times. So fixing our world-view and rejecting anything which threatens it is a surefire recipe for failure.

Uncertainty is uncomfortable, and adaptation is not easy or natural. As a result, we need inspiration and hope to fuel our enthusiasm for the difficult process of reassessing our beliefs and projections, risking new thoughts and actions, and adapting to constantly changing threats and circumstances. Despair and confusion are natural consequences of uncertainty and rapid change.

Thus the human mind needs inspiration and hope, which is why there is an insatiable demand for inspirational speakers and self-help books.

There are fundamentally two kinds of inspiration and hope; the simplistic kind, which has a half-life of about three days and is thus dissipated by Day Six, and the kind that is grounded on a realistic appraisal.

I'm going to present a variety of analogies throughout the book to help explain key concepts. If I use a cooking analogy, the meaning will be inaccessible to those who don't know how to cook. If I use a martial arts analogy, the meaning will be inaccessible to those who have never experienced rigorous mental and physical discipline. If I use trading examples, they will have no experiential meaning to those who haven't traded actively. To overcome the limitations of any one analogy, I will use a variety to reach as many different experiential backgrounds as possible.

So if one analogy doesn't resonate, keep reading—perhaps the next one will.

Since all of us have to eat, and most of us have a choice about what food we consume, then I'm going to start with the analogy of diet and health. What we choose to eat and what activities we choose bear directly on our well-being and our health. As Aristotle observed, "We are what we repeatedly do." This is "obvious," yet many of us find ourselves overweight and in poor health. Though the issue incorporates diet, nutrition, fitness and food preparation, it isn't limited to these "obvious" factors. It also incorporates two other sets of factors. One is the "ocean" we swim in: the way our society views food, diet, nutrition and fitness, and how our economy addresses the marketing of food and food services.

The second set of factors is internal: how we view our own body, the role eating plays in our family and inner life, our early experiences of food and fitness, the nature of self-discipline and instant gratification, and ultimately, our sense of self-worth and self-identity. Diet is not mechanical; it is a dynamic shaped by our environment even as it functions as a form of self-expression.

Investing and speculating are bound up with wealth and prosperity in the same way that diet and fitness are bound up with well-being and health. That's why the analogy of dieting is so powerful and practical as a way to understand the challenges of investing.

Since we're drawn to simple ideas and emotionally attractive messages of inspiration, then we are naturally drawn to simple diets and inspirational messages about dieting. This explains the endless appetite for new diets, new "miracle foods," and for dieting books, seminars and classes which inspire us with simple, easily digestible and emotionally appealing messages.

In the investing realm, this explains the insatiable appetite for thousands of books, articles, seminars, classes, newsletters and advisory services which purport to help us become wealthy.

What is remarkable about this intense interest and endless market for advice and inspiration is how few people ever lose weight and keep it off, and how few investors actually become wealthy by placing their faith in money managers or following investing advice. Indeed, 20-year studies have found that the number of investors, money managers and advisors who beat the S&P 500 index over both Bull and Bear markets is essentially zero—the equivalent of statistical noise.

Clearly, easily digestible guidelines and appealing inspirational messages aren't very effective in the real world when it comes to diet or investing.

Some might say that the advice was sound, and the failure of dieters and investors to lose weight/get rich resulted from their own lack of follow-through.

I would question this conclusion on several levels.

If an advisor really has a technique that works in the real world, then they should be able to turn $500 into $1,000,000 in only 11 good trades, or in 18 hedged trades.

Here is the math: if you double your capital in each trade, then $500 becomes $1,000,000 in only 11 trades. How many of those selling advice successfully turn $500 into $1,000,000 in a few trades? How many preserve that wealth over time?

A double isn't impossible when trading small-cap stocks (especially in the technology, commodity and biotechnology sectors), options or futures contracts. I have hit a number of 10-baggers (a 10-fold rise from the initial purchase price) and one 20-bagger in small-cap stocks, and I am just an amateur.

Last year I bought some option calls at $.52 on June 8th and sold them on June 10th for $1.09. Hordes of other traders have similar experiences. Is it guaranteed? No. Is it easy? No. Is it done on a regular basis? Yes. Options can double in two days; a volatile stock might take a year. But consistently doubling an investment is not impossible if your system actually works.

Here's how 11 good trades turn $500 into $1,000,000:
1) $500 becomes $1,000
2) $1,000 becomes $2,000
3) $2,000 becomes $4,000
4) $4,000 becomes $8,000
5) $8,000 becomes $16,000
6) $16,000 becomes $32,000
7) $32,000 becomes $64,000
8) $64,000 becomes $128,000
9) $128,000 becomes $256,000
10) $256,000 becomes $512,000
11) $512,000 becomes $1,064,000

One way to lower the risk of trading is to hedge the bet. For example, let's say you set aside 25% of your capital in every trade to buy "portfolio insurance" via a bet on the opposite side of the trade. Let's say you're 75% confident that oil will go up in the next few months, but to lower the risk of your trade losing value you allot 25% of your portfolio to a bet that oil will fall in price. This is in effect a hedge against the possibility that you are wrong.

So $1,000 becomes $1,500, as $750 doubles and the $250 portfolio insurance you bought is lost.

$1,500 becomes $2,250 as $375 is spent on "insurance," and so on. It now takes 18 trades to turn $500 into $985,261.

If a trading system actually worked with any sort of consistency in the real world, then anyone following the system should be able to turn $500 into $1,000,000 in 18 hedged trades. That so few do so—basically, statistical noise—and hold onto their wealth, is persuasive evidence that systems don't work consistently, and that following simple rules does not lead to consistent trading success.

The problem isn't just a lack of follow-through; simple nostrums don't work in the real world. Here are two examples: the way to make money in the market is buy low and sell high, and the way to lose weight is to consume fewer calories than you burn. Both are certainly true, but both are equally useless as advice because the hard part isn't the nostrum, it's the process of buying low and selling high or consuming fewer calories that turns out to be exceedingly difficult in the real world.

Moving one step beyond simple nostrums to simple systems: if their systems worked in the real world, then advisors would be able to publish a list of trades that turned $500 into $1,000,000. After all, how hard is it to string together 18 highly profitable trades in a row if your system really works?

I can't show you a list of 18 trades of mine that turned $500 into $1,000.000, but then I'm not selling a system or advice that claims to give you some sort of edge. I readily confess to be being one of the world's worst traders, and I have learned it is foolhardy for me to engage the market except in specific circumstances.

I recently came across an investment advice service which claimed, "Our system works as illustrated - every time - on any traded security, future or option that returns a high, low and close at close of trading of the market."

If I had such a foolproof, guaranteed system of trading to exploit, I certainly wouldn't share it for a few dollars a month: I would load up on highly-leveraged options and futures contracts at every signal and quickly mint a fortune.

This introduces what I call The Paradox of Trading Systems. The paradox has two parts: if a system really worked, then the owner would be insane to give it away for a few dollars a month. The second part is that no system works forever, and its transition from working to not working is not announced or telegraphed. Thus you can never know if a bad trade was the result of an outlier or if it is a sign that your system no longer works. That introduces the very uncertainty your system was designed to eliminate.

The same can be said of money managers and backtesting. The past performance of a money manager has little bearing on his or her future performance, because whatever intuitive or mechanical system the manager relies on will stop outperforming at an unknown point in time. If it were easy to mimic a trapeze artist and swing one's fortune to another money manager as soon as the previous one stopped outperforming, then we'd all be millionaires in short order. The evidence is unequivocal: nobody outperforms in the long run over both Bull and Bear markets. The only reliable prediction is that hot hands turn cold without warning.

Backtesting of trading systems is often presented as the "answer" to the question: does this system offer a measurable advantage over passive investing, i.e. putting all your money in index funds? But once again, backtesting is a metric of history, and projecting the past into the future introduces the very uncertainties that backtesting is supposed to eliminate. A system which worked in the past could stop working tomorrow or the next day, without warning. The more traders come to rely on the system for an advantage, the faster that advantage dissipates.

The same test can be run on diets and diet advice. The number of people who lose weight and remain trim five years later is remarkably small.

There is a great irony in all this. We want a simple, inspirational plan so badly that we ignore the fact that simple, inspirational plans fail in the real world.

If you are seeking a simple, inspirational message that is founded on false hope, you will not find it here. Reaping speculative gains and losing weight are both devilishly difficult in the real world.

The alternative kind of inspirational hope is one grounded in a realistic appraisal of the challenges we face, both external and internal. The "solution" isn't the new grapefruit diet: the only real solution is to explore the way we think about food, eating, diet, fitness, gratification and our own body, and slowly transform the way we think about them with new insights and new habits of thought and behavior.

In the investment world, the solution isn't a "secret technique" or investing in housing because "real estate never goes down;" it is understanding the financial world we swim in and our own conceptions of risk and prosperity.

This self-examination is often very painful, which is why we shy away from the process. Would you let a friend you care about eat the same way you do? If we care about our bodies, then why are we eating such unhealthy foods?

In the investment world, a similar question could be phrased: would you be as cavalier with a friend's money as you are with your own? What does your answer say about your awareness of risk?

Here is another analogy I hope you can relate to: the cheaply made martial arts film. (If you dislike this genre, please bear with me; another analogy will be along shortly.)

One of the staple plots of the martial arts genre is the "secret technique" which is generally illustrated in a scroll or book. This can be elaborated in various ways, for example, the illustration is invisible without some special treatment, a twist that flummoxes our hero/heroine after they finally obtain the scroll.

Our hero is always been bested by an evil opponent who has mastered martial arts without any visible training. Our hero's only hope to beat the evil master and save his family/fiancé/village/kingdom is to get his hands on the scroll and learn the secret technique.

Naturally, our hero only reaches the scroll after an arduous journey involving many thrills and spills, and he usually has only a moment to glance at the technique before unleashing it on his evil opponent. The "secret technique" might involve getting tipsy ("drunken master").

The same theater plays out in the investment and dieting realms; "secret techniques" or strategies are marketed as uniquely valuable, or at least more valuable than the wealth of information that's available for free on the Web. In the dieting/weight loss world, there are endlessly inventive yet somehow repetitive "miracle diets" and weight loss techniques.

Once again, the "secret technique" appeals to our innate preference for simplicity and emotional clarity.

The realities of sustained weight loss and martial arts are quite different from the promises of easy inspirational miracles. Before being shown a real martial arts technique, first you need to warm up for five minutes. Human nature being what it is, very few people would even last through the warm-up, never mind the lesson: we want the "secret technique" right now.

There is a "secret technique" in martial arts, one known to the ancient Taoists. Famed martial arts master Bruce Lee described it thusly: "A good martial artist does not become tense but ready. Not thinking yet not dreaming, ready for whatever may come. A martial artist has to take responsibility for himself and face the consequences of his own doing. To have no technique, there is no opponent, because the word 'I' does not exist. When the opponent expands, I contract and when he contracts, I expand. And when there is an opportunity, 'I' do not hit, 'It' hits all by itself."

If you substitute "trader" for "martial artist," and "trade" for "hit," then this quote offers a very useful guide to trading.

The secret technique is repetition of actions taken with what the Buddha called "right mindfulness" and what others might call self-awareness or impeccability. The Taoists celebrated butchers and bird-catchers, among others, as examples of those who through insight and practice have attained the spiritual level of skill that Bruce Lee described as a unity of awareness and reflex.

The connection between the discipline of martial arts and trading is more than mere fancy; an inordinate number of professional traders are also martial artists. It may be the competitive spirit of trading and martial arts attracts a certain personality, but the connection is not just a matter of individual character: making money in the market and mastering martial arts are equally difficult.

If the era we are entering is one of changing rules, disruptive endgames, and extremes of instability, then simply holding on to whatever wealth you have will be challenging. But if we just give up and trust in drifting with the Status Quo tides, then the likelihood of maintaining or growing our wealth drops significantly. Once again this parallels our diet/fitness/health analogy: when it comes to diet, fitness and health, we truly have no choice: if we give up the goals of pursuing our own well-being and health, then the most likely result is untimely death from one chronic disease or another.

In troubled times, passively hoping the Status Quo will preserve your wealth is akin to eating everything you want, whenever you want and hoping you'll end up slim and fit.

If all this chatter about martial arts seems esoteric and unrelated to investing in troubled times, the point is that great accomplishments (such as building wealth in troubled times or losing weight and becoming fit) come from simple behaviors that are repeated often enough that they forge new reflexive habits.

The way to lose weight is to condition oneself to enjoy a healthy diet and to walk every day. The way to make money in troubled times is to align your goals and rules with your character and situation, train yourself to see volatility as opportunity, use relative strength and hedging as guides, stay out of the market if there is no opportunity and embrace failure as your friend.

Unfortunately, there is no "secret technique" for investing, any more than there is a "magic diet" for losing weight. Any mechanical "one size fits all" system that produces outsized gains today will stop working at some point in the future, just as advice to "buy real estate" will only be appropriate for specific windows of time in specific markets.

In our hunter-gatherer analogy, the tree's fruit is only ripe at certain seasons; the rest of the time, the tree is barren.

Willpower or self-discipline is like a muscle—it becomes stronger with exercise over time, but it also tires when used repeatedly in a short period of time. This is one reason why we find it so difficult to lose weight: in exerting our willpower to exercise, our reserves of self-discipline are drained by the time we go to the café afterward. Then we order a coffee latte and a fat-and-sugar loaded muffin, and end up consuming twice as many calories as we burned.

If there is anything that approximates a "secret technique," it is self-knowledge. If we try to force ourselves to adopt an exercise regime or trading style that doesn't fit our core personality, we will tire of it as our willpower is drained. At that point, we will abandon it entirely.

Self-knowledge is very difficult and painful to attain, and that is why it is so devilishly difficult to lose weight or trade successfully.

Some of you may be shaking your head at the "obviousness" of this point, but those of you with more trading experience will be nodding your head in recognition.

Although we are programmed to think of martial arts as being about beating other people up, it is (as Bruce Lee observed) fundamentally a form of self-expression. The same can be said of trading and investing. As I said before, any enterprise is a form of self-expression. If it isn't, then it is doomed to fail because the environment is simply too unforgiving to reward half-hearted effort.

Traders often refer to the market as an opponent: the market will take your money at every opportunity, for example, or it will exploit your every weakness. What they're really referring to is the market provides us an opportunity to sabotage ourselves or create obstacles of our own design. The market enables us to choose a way of engaging it that doesn't align with our personality. Though we feel as though we're struggling against a demonic being that constantly confounds us, what we're really struggling against is ourselves and the way we've chosen (explicitly or by default) to engage the market.

In the weight loss/fitness analogy, many people view a healthy diet and exercise as a sacrifice or an onerous burden. Interestingly, they never seem to see putting unhealthy food in their bodies as a burden, or exercise as liberation and self-expression. The key is not self-discipline, though that is necessary; the key is transforming the way we experience our body, identity, gratification, meal preparation, fitness, self-management, self-understanding and our default habits and thoughts.

In the world of investing, we must transform our understanding of wealth, risk and speculation. In the era we are now entering, investing is an illusion: everything is a speculation, whether we accept it as such or not. Direct control of our assets will become a critical factor, for reasons I will explain later.

Buy-and-hold won't work in unstable, volatile times, and neither will counting on sideways or muddle-through markets. Putting your faith in those who rely on doing the same things they've been doing for the past 20 years isn't going to work, either.

All correlations, patterns and models are fundamentally based on past data. If the future unfolds in patterns which don't echo the past, then models based on the past will not help us anticipate the future.

I'm going to use a story as a metaphor for what I have to offer in the way of realistic inspiration and hope. A few years ago I taught our friends' young daughters how to ride their bicycles. I started with the older one and then repeated the process with her sister. My technique was simple: I began by steadying the bike's handlebar as the girl attempted to pedal forward and not topple over. I announced a goal: try to ride unassisted for three seconds. Despite her beginner's wobble, she managed to ride for three seconds while I walked alongside, at which point I again steadied the handlebar. I then set the next goal: ride unassisted for five seconds. After that success, the goal moved to ten seconds. By the time she'd ridden for ten seconds without falling over, her confidence rose, and she quickly reached the next goal of 20 seconds.

Within a few minutes, the girls were circling their driveway, amazed at how "easy" it was to learn how to ride a bicycle. Of course teaching them to safely navigate busy city streets took many hours and many long rides, but their initial confidence was instilled by this simple technique.

If you seek a fizzy sugar-high of inspiration, I have nothing to offer you. The road ahead is ridiculously difficult, and it will take all our courage, self-knowledge, skill and insight to build resilient households in the troubled times ahead. I believe that understanding offers us an enduring source of confidence and inspiration.

5 | The Unconventional Path

I wrote this book for four classes of people:

1) Those who have lost money on previous investments/bets and want to do better in the future.

2) Those who want to preserve what wealth they have now.

3) Those who want enough prosperity to be happy in the troubled times ahead.

The fourth class is one many people would avoid identifying with in public, but it includes a fair percentage of the human population:

4) Those who want to dramatically increase their wealth via the Black Arts of Speculation.

I think this covers close to 99% of humanity.

For those brave souls who confess to occasional desires for easy wealth via the Black Arts of Speculation: are you girding yourself for a stern lecture on the evils of greed? De-gird yourself. The desire for easy wealth is selected into the human animal, along with all other species. I call it *windfall exploitation,* and the desire to exploit any windfall that comes along has been an excellent survival strategy. As hunter-gatherers, when we came on a tree loaded with fruit, it aided our survival to exploit that windfall to the fullest.

So the fact that the human race seeks to exploit any windfall—i.e. get filthy stinking rich with the least possible effort—makes perfect sense.

That a certain level of prosperity is the foundation of happiness needs no explanation. But what sort of wealth and what level of prosperity is required for happiness/fulfillment requires some exploration. For it may well be that playing the stock/bond/commodities/foreign exchange markets actively obstructs accumulation of wealth and serves to distract us from true prosperity and happiness. Rather than being the engine of wealth we all desire—the windfall we all seek--the markets may be sources of entirely counterproductive anxiety, fear and loss.

There is no "one size fits all" investment scheme that makes sense to the full spectrum of potential situations and personalities. What I hope to present here is a perspective on investing that offers a useful foundation for your own research and analysis.

Yes, *your* analysis and decisions. There is only one person qualified to make your financial decisions for you, and that person is you.

I have divided this into two parts: the first will address the psychology of investing (speculation) and the second will cover some basic tools to help you choose a strategy which fits your personality and situation.

There is no "easy way to wealth," there is only selecting a path that's easier for you to stay on, i.e. an approach that aligns with your personality, strengths, weaknesses and goals. Self-knowledge is never easy, but it is always rewarding.

But before we begin, I need to explain a few things about the format and content of this guide. I include no charts or graphs, because all of that material is available in hundreds of other investment-related books, or on the Web. Furthermore, any chart or graph I did include would instantly be outdated and thus possibly misleading. I also don't try to explain technical analysis, as that too has been exhaustively explored in hundreds of other books and in thousands of web pages. I have endeavored to write a guide that is accessible to both those who are new to investing and those with experience who are interested in an unconventional perspective. To keep the book from becoming an encyclopedia, I am relying on your curiosity to lead you to other sources on the Web and in libraries.

The goal here is to describe dynamics and perspectives that are not found in all the other investment guides, many of which are never voiced lest the writer's own livelihood in the investing game be undermined.

We should start every inquiry with the question: *cui bono*, to whose benefit? The psychology of any confidence game ("con") is to persuade the mark (victim) that the game is to their benefit, when in reality the game is rigged to benefit the "house" or con artist.

The status quo centralized global market is confidence game, and thus the one essential task is to convince you that playing the game benefits you. In certain circumstances, it might benefit you, but this is quite different than claiming "buy and hold for the long-term" is in your best interest. In long Bull markets this is true, but not true in long Bear markets, or periods of volatility or stagflation.

I do not have any investment newsletter or portfolio management service to sell. I gain nothing from your belief in the conventional investment world or your rejection of it except the modest sum earned from the sale of this book. Given the amount of time and experience it took to write this book, it is unlikely that I will earn a return on my investment much above minimum wage.

I am an outsider and thus have no stake in maintaining the artifice of "transparent markets" and no incentives to keep quiet about the fraud, manipulation, collusion, embezzlement, accounting trickery, shadow systems and misrepresentation of risk which are now the business model of the U.S. financial system.

The conventional investing world is adamantly apolitical; the desire to profit from addiction, warfare and other scourges on humanity is flaunted as a point of pride: maximizing profit, we are repeatedly assured, is all that matters, and if the corporate pusher of addiction makes you more money than other options, then you are a chump if you don't invest in the pusher.

I reject this apolitical obsession with maximizing profits as the only metric of "success." From my perspective, everything has a meta-level *politics of experience*, and thus every participant in the market is complicit in the system's fraud, embezzlement, misrepresentation of risk and collusion. Rather than the prideful profiteers they claim to be, participants are the chumps because the liquidity they provide via their investments is precisely what enables the skimming and manipulation of those holding asymmetrical knowledge and power within the markets.

If investors lose faith in the market and stops participating, then the cons will only have each other to con.

This is another advantage of guerrilla investing: not only does it lessen risk by staying out of the markets most of the time, but it also removes liquidity. From the point of view of insiders, your role in the market is to provide the liquidity they need to churn and skim, and to be the mark who buys the risk and future loss they are selling.

Taking a position in the market is a vote in favor of the Status Quo corruption, and every decision to withdraw capital from the market is a vote against the Status Quo. Thus the apolitical stance is pure illusion: our investments either support the Status Quo or they weaken it.

Small investors have been voting against the Status Quo by withdrawing tens of billions of dollars from domestic mutual funds during the 2009-2011 stock market rally: they didn't trust the rally or its cheerleaders, for good reasons.

The financial Status Quo insists that keeping your money invested in their game is in your best interests, but this assertion masks the ugly reality: your real role is to provide the liquidity for their profitable churn, and to buy the risk and future losses from insiders. If we are aware of this reality, it informs our basic strategy: only take a position when the risk-return is overwhelmingly advantageous (and by definition, disadvantageous to those on the other side of the trade).

Despite the systemic corruption and asymmetric risk, the markets, if carefully played, can offer outsiders an occasional opportunity or hedge. This summation has been attributed to General Douglas MacArthur: *"There is no security on this earth; there is only opportunity."* We can choose to enter the market, alert to its risks, or we can choose the safer path and avoid it altogether. If we do choose to enter, it is our duty to understand the many layers of risk.

6 | The Many Layers of Risk

The conventional investment world gives lip service to risk, but then quickly assures us it can be hedged or massaged away. This is the fundamental misrepresentation of risk that is used to snare credulous investors. Risk cannot be massaged away: all else is illusion. Everything is contingent and subject to unexpected instability.

Risk is inherently difficult to assess because it resides in our own minds and emotions as well as in the real world; humans are not constructed to act in a fool-proof fashion when faced with risk. We have been selected to make quick intuitive decisions when facing danger. Alternatively, we "freeze up" when overwhelmed by unfamiliar situations and sensory overload, or default to a "follow the herd" risk-management strategy, as there is safety in numbers in many threatening situations.

Put another way: risk is not just in the market, it's within us, as our self-awareness in risky circumstances is remarkably low for a good reason: over the past 200,000 years when the human genome was relentlessly pressured by multiple threats, self-awareness didn't serve us as well as following the herd or reacting intuitively.

Thus there are two sets of risks we face, one that is intrinsic to the human mind and a second set that is intrinsic to the market itself. The first set of risks has spawned a vast industry that explores the behavioral and cognitive psychology of investing.

This industry rests on an implicit assumption that all our built-in behavioral and cognitive traps can be skirted, and that skirting them will lead to consistent outperformance (i.e. getting filthy stinking rich). Put another way: once we bypass these built-in biases, then the road to riches is wide open.

This explains the great popularity of this industry and its assumption, which acts as yet another highly marketable source of simplistic hope and inspiration.

A more cynical view is that the markets are rigged against individual investors, and the claim that cognitive biases are the source of your underperformance is misleading.

The second set of risks poses a potentially fatal threat to the conventional investment world, for if people really understood that risk can never be massaged away, it can only be masked temporarily, they might not be so willing to risk their capital in the market.

Let's cover the second set of market-based risks, and then move on to so-called cognitive biases.

In essence, we take on far more risk than we recognize every time we enter a market. The idea that there are "safe" investments or "safe" hedges is illusory. The risk has not been eliminated; it has only been obscured. For more on this subject, please read the book *The (Mis)Behavior of Markets* by mathematician Benoit Mandelbrot.

In a nutshell, what Mandelbrot addresses is the uncanny knack of supposed rare events like market crashes, which are supposed to happen once every few generations, to actually occur every few years.

In a similar fashion, all the hedges which are supposed to reduce risk to near-zero manage to fail spectacularly with unsettling unpredictability, and yet they manage to do so with remarkable reliability.

In *Survival+* I suggest starting each inquiry by asking *cui bono*—to whose benefit? The answers to that question reveal that systems and concepts presented as either timeless truths or of benefit to all are actually carefully assembled misrepresentations designed to mask a highly self-serving reality.

If we ask *cui bono* of standard portfolio management and standard investment managers, newsletters, etc., in light of Mandelbrot's mathematical insights into the regularity of meltdowns, then we reach an uncomfortable answer: everyone with a stake in the "game" has a powerful reason--self-interest--to mask, discredit or discount the reality that risk cannot be massaged away.

Why is this so? For the simple reason that if everyone who was considering putting their money at risk knew the risks were intrinsically high at all times, and that "lowering risk" through "prudent risk management" was intrinsically illusory—a misleadingly thin layer of chocolate icing smoothed over toxic truths—then very few would be willing to accept those high risks for the modest returns offered by those skimming money from the game as managers or advisors.

In other words, masking the impossibility of reducing risk is a highly profitable business.

If everyone decided to walk away from such an unfavorable risk-return scenario, the tens of thousands of people skimming vast sums of money from the implicit promise of financial alchemy—turning high-risk lead into low-risk gold—would be out of a job.

This is not to say there aren't many conscientious souls within the money-management industry who are trying to preserve their clients' capital and make them money in lower-risk, higher-return investments; there are many such people. My point is systemic: anyone who keeps their clients' money in cash for very long will be fired, because the money-management industry profits from churn (buying and selling), the creation and marketing of "low risk, high yield" investments and the selling of hedges for "portfolio protection."

Indeed, the entire global financial meltdown of 2008 can be traced to financial instruments that were sold as "low risk, high yield" investments or hedges rather than what they really were: high-risk, low yield gambles that were extremely vulnerable to implosion. That reality had to be masked to make the highly profitable sale to credulous investors.

There is another set of risks that are brushed aside or discounted by the conventional money-management industry: systemic risks that are outside the boundaries of standard risk-management and outside the worldview of those benefiting from the financialization machine of crony-capitalist, monopoly-cartel Neoliberal Global Capitalism. These systemic risks include destabilizing disruptions in the global supply lines of energy, structural imbalances in global finance and political upheavals that could fatally disrupt the financial networks on which the money-management system depends.

These systemic risks are a problem for conventional portfolio management because 1) their consequences are unpredictable; 2) they are difficult to hedge and 3) they are disruptive and could spell the end of the system which tens of thousands of people depend on for their livelihood.

All markets, from neighborhood swap meets to global markets, require several conditions: transparency (or the illusion of transparency), the active participation of buyers and sellers, and abundant liquidity, i.e. money available as a means of exchange and plenty of supply and demand (bids and asks) to fuel numerous transactions.

If a market loses any of these, it quickly declines. People soon abandon a rigged game, and once participation falls then remaining buyers and sellers find the number of potential customers falls below a critical threshold. The market becomes illiquid, i.e. there are few buyers or sellers so prices become volatile and can be pushed into cliff-dive cascades by relatively few participants. As participants abandon the market, a self-reinforcing feedback (positive feedback) takes hold; as people leave, those who had been clinging on hoping for a return of the good old days throw in the towel.

We can see this dynamic in the housing market, which is still in the post-bubble decline phase. The housing market reached bubble valuations as more renters were enabled to buy houses by easy credit and low interest rates, and the market was expanded by all those lured by the windfalls of rapidly rising prices into buying and selling ("flipping") homes.

As credit tightened and prices fell, the windfalls disappeared, and so did participation. As the first wave of cash investors "buying the bottom" receded, there were few qualified buyers left and a surplus of inventory on the market. Prices continued falling as houses languished for months and buyers' low bids were eventually accepted. Once the fantasy of "easy profits from flipping real estate" is finally extinguished, then participation will decline further.

There is another risk to market participants, a fundamentally political one: as my blogging colleague Jesse of Jesse's Café Americain observed: "Oligarchies spread only the risks, while keeping most of the benefits to themselves." In my view, the financial Oligarchy has partnered with the Central State and bank; others see the State and central bank as captured by the financial cartel. The primary point is the market is not transparent; rather, it is a carefully engineered web of shadow institutions, opaque self-serving (you buy newly issued Treasury bonds and the Federal Reserve buys them one minute later for a premium, thereby allowing the Fed to claim it doesn't buy Treasury bonds directly), favoritism, protected vested interests, embezzlement, fraud, misrepresentation of risk (this security is rated AAA, etc.), lax oversight, near-zero accountability, regulations that go unenforced as a matter of unstated policy, bogus accounting and ultimately, the transfer of private risk to the public coffers.

Thus participants will shoulder outsized losses as markets destabilize, while the financial cartels will simply transfer their losses to the public sector (taxpayers). In sum: despite claims to the contrary, the risk is asymmetrically high to investors and low to Oligarchies, a reality that is masked by a veneer of transparency designed to pull in credulous marks.

In the developed world, Central States that have overpromised entitlements to their citizens and corporate "partners" (the cartels which dominate the developed economies) will be forced to confiscate more of their productive citizens' wealth and revenues. The consumer nations such as the U.S. have spent more than their economy has produced, and they've filled the gap between consumption and production with debt. The debt must be serviced, of course, and that only further widens the gap between spending and revenues.

As a result, Central States will find it increasingly appealing to impose a "state of emergency" which includes direct confiscation or confiscation by other means such as a television tax, a wealth tax, windfall tax, etc. As noted above, it costs very little for the State to collect these taxes via centralized authorities, and so there are major incentives to skim from those who are powerless to evade the State's reach: for example, employees whose wages are subject to withholding, those with their money in banks, pensioners who received checks from the State, and so on.

The immensely wealthy Elites' political power will buy exemptions from this confiscation; the self-employed have fewer options than the super-wealthy Power Elites, but small enterprises will probably continue to have more legal ways to protect their income than employees.

One under-appreciated way to avoid some of these taxes is to live in such a way that your expenses are very low. The Central State is careful not to drive its low-income citizens to open political rebellion, which is why it provides bread and circuses (food stamps, free TV, etc.) that cost a small fraction of total government expenditures. Since it cannot heavily tax people with very little income without inciting potentially destabilizing blowback, then having a low income will likely remain a refuge from the relentless expansion of State confiscation.

Alternatively, you can amass $100 million or so and join the spirited bidding for elected officials who will exempt your fortune, or you can become politically engaged and join others seeking to limit the private concentration of power and wealth that fuels the State's centralization of power.

7| Novelty, Habit and Cognitive Biases

If we had to distill human nature down to a series of eternally conflicting forces, we might start with the traditional moral duality of good and evil. I would start any exploration of investing with our dueling desires for novelty and habit. We constantly seek the excitement of novelty, yet we also find security in well-worn routines and habits that have served us well.

The evolutionary benefit of these opposing traits is clear: a pleasure in novelty takes us over the hill to see what's on the other side and keeps us alert for windfalls. Novelty can be dangerous, too, of course, and exploring requires major investments in energy and time—investments which might not pay off. So low-risk, low-cost routines offer a security and emotional respite from the rigors of seeking out novelty.

The attraction to novelty is akin to that of windfalls, and this is visible in our willingness to follow up a "hot tip" on a stock that might yield a windfall (big profits) even though our lack of information poses a great risk. We tend to churn our accounts because we seek new investments (novelty) that promise a windfall. Yet we also stick to the same paths out of habit, and resist anything which threatens our time-honored routines and beliefs.

Many legendary investors have commented on the wisdom of holding onto positions until the trend ends. Financial media stories often include references to the fantastic gains reaped by anyone who bought Microsoft in 1986, for example, and held it to 2000. Very few investors did so, of course, largely because there was no novelty in owning Microsoft for 14 years.

The attraction of established routine is visible in those who continue playing in markets that are going down; it's as if they cannot bear to leave the playing field but would rather stay and play even if they're losing. Habit and resistance to change are powerful attractors, even when they serve us poorly.

Though gains and profit are supposedly the sole motivation for playing the market, this is only the surface motivation. Deep within us are other conflicting forces.

Some of these have been cordoned off and labeled "cognitive biases" in the popular financial media. I am skeptical of the value of this approach, starting with the negative connotations of the word "bias," which trivializes the human mind and natural selection.

If you run a web search on "cognitive biases," you will find the list is astonishingly long and varied. Here is an abridged list:

1) Anchoring Trap: Relying on first thoughts or impressions

2) Status Quo Trap: It's comfortable to maintain the status quo and avoid change

3) Sunk Cost Trap: Protecting earlier investments/choices

4) Confirmation Trap: Selecting data to support your point of view

5) Incomplete Information Trap: Making decisions on incomplete information

6) The Conformity Trap: Following the herd

7) The Illusion of Control Trap: We love to feel in control even when we're not

8) The Coincidence Trap: We confuse probability, coincidence and our intuitive sense

9) The Recall Trap: We over-emphasize high-impact events in selective memory

10) The Superiority Trap: We overestimate our skills and capabilities

There is even a cognitive bias to describe how those who grossly over-estimate their knowledge and skill level are prone to not even realizing the true paucity of their knowledge and skills.

Here are a few more biases:

11) Hindsight Trap: Since we understand the past, we can also understand the future

12) Extrapolation Trap: Current trends will continue into the future

13) The "I can overcome cognitive biases" trap (OK, I just made this one up)

If you try to banish confirmation bias from your thinking, you may be indulging in four or five other cognitive biases of which you are not even aware. That would be dangerous because then you would be over-estimating your lack of biases.

Is there any useful insight on investing in this approach, or is it just another variation of fizzy, appealing pop psychology—that is, the promise of fundamental transformation via cheap nostrums?

If the primary source of our lack of success is cognitive bias, and all we had to do to eliminate cognitive bias from our investing/trading was read a book, then there would be massive crowds of self-made millionaires congratulating themselves on the remarkable profits gains from eliminating cognitive bias.

But there are no such crowds of milling millionaires. From my perspective, what others label "cognitive biases" are complex, highly beneficial heuristics that have been selected over countless generations for their great value. To claim that these "biases" are impediments is to completely miss the point: no heuristic or intuitive algorithm works well in every situation, yet this is the implicit claim of those who set great store in "cognitive biases." In other words, if a heuristic fails in any circumstance, it is arbitrarily labeled a "cognitive bias," even if works to our favor much of the time.

A more insightful approach is to get rid of "cognitive biases" as a misleading category, and view the selected heuristics of the human mind as analytical short-cuts which compete in the subconscious with one another for practical value in a form of natural selection.

It is certainly wise to be aware of the way these intuitive short-cuts color our consciousness and emotions, but to claim that they must be overcome is to misunderstand their utility. There is no "good" or "bad" heuristic, there are only more or less appropriate heuristics. To think you can eliminate "cognitive biases" and have anything useful remaining is to completely misunderstand the human mind and set up a counterproductive expectation.

There are other problems with the "cognitive bias" approach to "making you a profitable investor." These books and articles are long on lists and short on describing the precise process one can use to eliminate or master one's "cognitive biases." Without such a description, then all the lists of "cognitive biases" boil down to empty nostrums that are the equivalent of "buy low, sell high": the slogan itself is valueless, as only the process of identifying the buys and sells has value.

From the point of view of natural selection, every "bad" cognitive heuristic "bias" is also "good" in some circumstances.

There is an even deeper layer of risk which is as firmly grounded in natural selection. Risk is intimately bound up with feelings of power and exhilaration because at one level, risk is power. Taking risk is a strategy which offers competitive advantages in the search for resources and mates—the "winnings" which evolution selects for over the generations. Those who "win" the most/best mates and garner the most resources to care for their offspring will be more successful in passing on their genes and behavioral traits. Competing for resources and mates requires risk. Those with little appetite for risk may well survive, but the willingness to take on risk offers competitive advantages powerful enough that this willingness to accept risk is itself selected as advantageous.

We are often told that risk is "bad," but just as with cognitive heuristics, the willingness to take on risk is neither "good" or "bad"—it has potential downside and potential upside. Risk is ever-present, and doing nothing can be just as risky as taking action.

From an evolutionary perspective, what's selected as advantageous is the ability to differentiate between low-risk, high-return situations and high-risk, low-return situations. Since we possess self-awareness and conscious analytic skills, then we are not limited to our genome and the behaviors it favors. We can seek out heuristic short-cuts and tools that help us make this differentiation.

8 | Self-Knowledge and the Psychology of Investing

For many, the ideal investing strategy or system is purely mechanical, that is, a set of rules which can be programmed into a computer and executed without human decision. This is seen as the ideal solution because it removes "the human factor" and the potential for human error from the process.

Mechanical rules are "one size fits all": they work the same for anyone in any setting. This is their advantage.

Others have noted that mechanical systems have limits; they tend to stop outperforming over time and have to be constantly modified. If their programmed models of risk and return fail, then losses result.

For still others, the solution is to leverage what psychologists have learned about human behavior and cognitive foibles: broadly speaking, the psychology of investing. This boils down to understanding cognitive and emotional biases and seeking to overcome them. Once again, this is a "one size fits all" idea: we all share the same cognitive biases.

What I notice separates very successful investors from "the rest of us" is not their use of mechanical rules or their knowledge of cognitive biases; it's their self-awareness and self-knowledge. They aren't fighting themselves, or thrashing about constantly changing strategies and systems. They are interested in becoming a better investor and in the process of investing, not just the goal of making money. They enjoy the process of looking for opportunities, and the process of studying and modifying their system or approach.

The analogy in diet/fitness is the person whose goal is to become healthier and happier as opposed to the person whose goal is to lose 10 pounds. The person who focuses only on losing 10 pounds tends to become frustrated with the process, to do battle with themselves and constantly switch plans and diets.

It seems to me that "one size fits all" mechanical rules and cognitive biases are only half of the equation: the other half is self-awareness and self-knowledge of the individual. In other words, this other half is knowledge that is unique to a single individual.

This may seem self-evident and of little value.

It is difficult to discuss concepts that are self-evident because their very self-evidence demotes them to "obvious," a state of mind where they are dismissed as ordinary. As a result, I approach this most fundamental issue within the psychology of investing with great trepidation, for it seems too obvious to not only be profound but profoundly useful.

Our trust in "one size fits all" mechanical systems is grounded in the enormous success these systems have achieved in the modern era.

The biomedical and industrial revolutions of the past 100 years were both based on what we might characterize as the "one size fits all" model. In medicine, the great advances of antibiotics and inoculation were successful because they worked equally well in virtually all humans. The human body was understood as a biological machine whose inner workings were shared by all; individual variations had little effect, as only a small handful of individuals responded adversely to inoculation or antibiotics.

In a similar fashion, mass production of identical products enabled the consumer society, and the "factory model" of education provided a production-line institution to "manufacture" an educated populace with three basic "product lines": below average, average and above average.

At this point it is instructive to return to our diet/fitness analogy, for the basis of diets and fitness programs is that "one size fits all"—the same diet (or fitness program) will work equally well for everyone. In a sense, this is an extension of the Factory Model: the overweight, unfit person is issued a set of rules to follow, and the results (weight loss and improved fitness) will be, if not identical, then uniformly successful.

Yet observation shows that very few people lose weight and keep it off over the long term, and very few improve their fitness and retain this improved fitness over the long term.

The Factory Model doesn't work when it comes to weight loss and fitness, and increasingly, many question whether it produces the sort of education we need in a post-industrial economy. The only program with a long-term track record of results in weight reduction is Weight Watchers, which is built on a model that requires daily monitoring of food consumption, a choice of foods within clearly defined limits, and the emotional support provided by a group of people who share the same goal.

A more unconventional view of diet and fitness is that change requires a transformation of understanding founded not just on a sound grasp of nutrition and fitness (that is, "one size fits all" models) but on self-knowledge and a set of goals and rules which are tailored to the unique personality of the individual. This is the exact opposite of the "one size fits all" model.

From this perspective, the starting point is an individual establishes a goal with enduring meaning to that individual. The foundation of the process is self-knowledge, so that the diet and fitness rules are aligned with the individual's character and conditioning. Discipline is necessary until new habits of thought and behavior are established via repetition, but the fundamental transformation is a new understanding of three factors: the unique mix of conditioning and character that make up the individual; the nature and meaning of food, fitness and well-being to that individual, and the nature and meaning of the process of self-knowledge to the individual.

The transformation is not so much the following of a set of "one size fits all" rules as it is focusing on the process of becoming healthy and formulating a set of rules which align with one's character so they become part of one's understanding, routines and life. The idea isn't imposing a set of rules on someone, rather like a machine stamping out a template, but the individual exploring what works best for them.

Diets are generally viewed as deprivation, i.e. the painful sacrifice of foregoing desired foods such as ice cream and pizza. Deprivation and suffering are not positive long-term motivators, and so it is no surprise that diets based on a sense of deprivation fail.

In a more unconventional approach, the individual no longer wants to burden themselves with unhealthy doses of ice cream and pizza, and rather than seeing exercise as some sort of punishment, the individual now misses exercise the way they once missed ice cream.

Deprivation, sacrifice and suffering have lost their foothold in this new understanding, and so there are fewer sources of resistance and self-sabotage. The goals, processes and habits become self-sustaining because they arise from a self-awareness that is aligned with the individual's character.

Though we all share the same spectrum of human traits and eat from the same range of foods, the goals and set of rules which work for us is unique to us. Various regimes, rules and plans can act as starting points, but the working set of rules must fit our goals, our conditioning, our personality: ultimately, as with martial arts or any art, they operate as self-expression.

This is also true when it comes to investing.

The conventional investing model is based on the idea that all you need to do to become successful investor is to follow a set of rules which will work with equally positive results for all users. If these models worked, then everyone who received their cognitive bias inoculation and Secret Technique would be minting millions in the market. But there is scant evidence these models work. As noted before, the number of investors and managers who beat passive investing (index funds) over both Bull and Bear markets is essentially zero/statistical noise.

If any set of rules worked for everyone in all settings, then anyone with $500 would be a millionaire in 11 unhedged trades or 18 hedged trades by simply mechanically following the rules.

The conventional model presumes that only two things stand between the average investor and the one who mints millions: a set of easily grasped "one size fits all" investing rules and a technique to overcome cognitive biases.

There are tools which can help us become better investors, but it's not a lack of rules which inhibit our success. One size does not fit all. The choice of where and how to invest one's three forms of capital—human, social and financial—is the key to investing success, and the foundation of that choice is self-knowledge.

In this view, self-knowledge, which is *a priori* unique to each individual, is the single most important key to investing success. Conventional investing advice views the individual in the same light as cognitive biases, as the problem which stands in the way of the solution, which is a universal application of standardized rules. In other words, if only we could become machines, then we could all become extremely successful traders.

In my view, this is entirely backwards. The promise that mastering "one size fits all" techniques and inoculations against cognitive bias will inevitably lead to outperformance is demonstrably false. Observation of successful investors leads us to a different conclusion: success lies down the uniquely individual path of self-knowledge, which can only be gained by self-observation, self-awareness, trial and error and self-forgiveness.

Self-knowledge and self-expression are two aspects of the same source of insight.

The idea that financial success—what might be called "financial fitness"--stems from self-expression is completely alien to the conventional investing perspective. Yet how can the way we live and invest be anything but self-expression?

Let's cut through the confusion with a simple question: what is stopping each of us from becoming a millionaire? It isn't capital, because $500 can be turned into $1 million in only 11 trades. It also isn't a lack of tools, techniques or strategies. If the hundreds of books on investing really provided a set of rules that worked (i.e. led to outperformance over both Bull and Bear markets) and that anyone could follow, then anyone who read the books would soon be a millionaire, just as anyone who read a diet book would be slim and fit.

Yet the number of people who become millionaires (and stay millionaires) from reading investment books is remarkably small, roughly comparable to the number of people who become slim and fit (and stay slim and fit) from reading books on diet and fitness. From this we can conclude that a lack of "one size fits all" investing guidelines and diets is not the problem, and that the difficulty lies elsewhere.

What separates those who are healthy and fit from those who are not, and those who are successful investors from those who are not successful? It would be convenient if we could attribute the difference to genetics, but the observation suggests that the successful investors follow a set of rules which is easy for them to follow because it aligns with their personalities. They aren't fighting themselves every step of the way; they are exerting effort and practicing discipline, but they are doing so with the enthusiasm of self-expression.

I know several extremely successful individual investors who trade solely on their own account, that is, they are not professionals nor do they manage other people's money. There are as many ways to be a successful investor, i.e. preserve or grow one's capital and purchasing power, as there are individuals. There is no "one size fits all" technique or strategy. One individual I know has made over $1 million in a few years by following a set of rules that he developed for himself. I will explain his technique, but I doubt many people would be able to follow it over time because it was designed to align with this character and disposition.

This investor only trades a short list of silver stocks he has followed for years. When one stock in the list drops below its peers, he buys a substantial position in it. When it rises 1% or 2% then he sells it for a profit. The same technique could be used to skim profits from modest declines.

That is his technique, and he has made a small fortune from it. Successful investors, just like people who remain fit, are always tracking and modifying their results and rules. This is an integral part of their process. It isn't burdensome to them, it's challenging and fun.

My point is there is no "one size fits all" investment strategy or technique. The "successful" set of rules and strategy is the one which you can adhere to consistently and which produces positive results over the long term—in other words, one that you have developed to align with your goals, personality and situation.

There are many books on the psychology of investing, most of which straddle the notion that if only we could rid ourselves of troublesome emotional and cognitive biases, we would become successful traders and investors. In other words, the point of self-knowledge is to identify and then overcome these emotional and cognitive biases.

Legendary trader Ed Seykota summed up the psychology of investing this way: "Win or lose, everybody gets what they want out of the market. Some people seem to like to lose, so they win by losing money."

That we might want to lose money is difficult for most of us to accept: why would we want to lose? I can think of a number of reasons why an individual might subconsciously choose to lose money:

1. I deserve to lose, i.e. I am not truly worthy of finance success.

2. I am conditioned to stress and want, and financial security makes me uncomfortable.

3. Between having to admit a mistake or losing money, the less painful choice is to lose money.

4. The excitement of high risk is more enjoyable than profiting from "boring" trades.

5. I aspire to the godlike status of taking on impossible odds and "winning."

6. I feel impulsiveness is "authentic," while control and discipline are "suppressing our true selves."

7. Losing is what motivates me; when I "win," I lose my *joie de vivre* and drive.

8. Wealth is a burden and so getting rid of it is an emotional relief.

9. Wealth is essentially evil, and my spiritual purity requires me to be poor.

10. I prefer rebellion to compliance, and losing is a form of rebellion.

These are just a few possibilities; the only person who can really know what you might have been conditioned to think and feel is you. Successful investing requires profound self-knowledge.

All great investors are keenly aware of the critical role psychology plays in investing/trading, and their advice invites us to explore possible barriers within ourselves. Here are a few examples of Mr. Seykota's guidelines:

"The elements of good trading are cutting losses, cutting losses, and cutting losses."

"Whatever you put your mind to, whatever you expect, be it positive or negative, you tend to draw into your life."

"Here's the essence of risk management: Risk no more than you can afford to lose, and also risk enough so that a win is meaningful. If there is no such amount, don't play."

"The feelings we accept and enjoy rarely interfere with trading."

Mr. Seykota has expressed the same point I am trying to make in a slightly different manner: "I don't think traders can follow rules for very long unless they reflect their own trading style. Eventually, a breaking point is reached and the trader has to quit or change, or find a new set of rules he can follow. This seems to be part of the process of evolution and growth of a trader."

If I had to characterize the psychology of investing in one phrase, I would paraphrase Mr. Seykota: the issue isn't managing your investments, it's managing yourself while you manage your investments.

Conventional investing advice implies that successful investing requires overcoming deeply pernicious emotional and cognitive biases. But this misses the reason why investing success is so rare. The solution is not so much to root out emotional and cognitive biases as it is to align one's habits with one's personality so that the focus is on self-knowledge rather than following some "one size fits all" set of rules.

Fitness and diet once again offer a practical analogy. Just as investing boils down to finding a set of goals and rules that align with your personality, fitness boils down to finding forms of exercise that are enjoyable and can thus be readily adapted as habits.

"One size fits all" diets or investment rules end up being frustrating, for we inevitably fail to follow rules which don't match our own personality and situation. The solution—a focus on self-knowledge, on monitoring our behavior and results, and on adapting and modifying our rules and habits—requires effort and insight. But the opportunity to do so is present for everyone.

Truth is often painful, and so naturally we shy away from it. Successful investors and entrepreneurs see failure as a friend and teacher. In private, successful investors will note that most people are envious of their success, but very few are interested in the learning the mechanics of their success.

We all want a simple set of rules to follow, just as we seek hope and inspiration. We all want to know the "secret to your success" as long as it's easy. The interviewer always asks the 110-year old for "the secret to your long life." We hope for an answer we can all follow, such as "I take a single shot of whiskey every night."

Though we all seek a simple, painless set of rules to follow, there is no such thing. The secret to someone else's investing success won't work for us; we each have to fashion our own individual path. We can learn from others' examples, but "cut and paste" only goes so far.

All this may strike you as too generalized to be useful, but that is the nature of gaining self-awareness: the process is unique to each person.

As a generalization, the process usually seems to include these steps:

1) Set realistic, concrete goals.

2) Monitor one's thoughts, feelings and progress via self-observations that are logged/ written down.

3) Focus on the process of self-awareness: "catching oneself in the act," asking questions of oneself and writing down the answers.

4) Trial and error: learning from failure, adapting, innovating: fail fast, fail small, fail often.

5) Practicing self-forgiveness. Our culture implicitly holds up perfection as a model, yet perfection is unrealistic. Even the very

best investors are wrong much of the time.

6)   The joys of insight and self-expression.

Just as nobody knows how the future will unfold, nobody knows what is best for someone else.

What we seek as traders, in Harun's words, is a consistent uptrend in ourselves as traders.

SECTION TWO
The Spectrum of Potential Investments

Just as visible light occupies only a small sliver of the entire electromagnetic spectrum, the conventional view of investing is limited to a narrow band of global financial choices: domestic and international stocks, corporate and government bonds, foreign currencies, etc. As noted above, in terms of correlation, these choices can be grouped as a single trade, and thus much of conventional "diversification" is largely illusory.

The profusion of exchange-traded funds (ETFs) in commodities and precious metals has offered some diversification from paper (fiat-currency) financial assets, but if the global or domestic financial system becomes destabilized, these financial instruments could be adversely affected, and that diversification would be nullified.

Thus diversification must be viewed not just as a choice of sectors or asset classes, but as a choice between those assets you control (decentralized, local) and those you don't control (global, centralized). Since most of us need income, then we can also distinguish between assets that may retain their purchasing power but which do not generate income, and those that generate income streams.

Since no one knows the future, keeping an unblinking eye on risk and diversifying capital across the spectrum of potential investments loom large as key strategies.

A key tenet of this book is that putting all three types of capital (human, social and financial) to work across the entire spectrum of investment will lower risk via diversification and thus improve returns. The ideal investment is one that is low cost- low risk that may yield outsized returns. The ideal investment strategy is an entrepreneurial one that shifts capital from low productivity enterprise (what might be called under-performing assets) to higher productivity enterprise (assets that are set to outperform).

The conventional investment worldview is that you need a professional money manager or advisor to handle your investments because the issues are now too complex for average mortals to understand.

In my view, investing is a form of self-expression and self-leadership, and so handing one's investment decisions to someone else is akin to having someone else pick your mate, your job and your home for you.

We all want a simple, painless decision process, as the human mind recoils from uncertainty and indecision. Having someone else decide for us certainly relieves the indecision, but as Eric Fromm observed in his seminal book *Escape From Freedom*, having others decide for you is just another form of tyranny.

Once we truly grasp the risks embedded in the centralized global financial system, then that system can no longer be perceived as a "safe and permanent" market. It is instead viewed more realistically as one whose chief advantage is liquidity, suitable only for placing hedges and short-term "guerrilla trades" that take advantage of extremes of relative valuation.

Risk is ever-present and so there is a spectrum of risks alongside the spectrum of investment options. In this section, I will cover this spectrum of risks, many of which are unique to specific investments, and then cover each class of investments within the broad spectrum of options. Many of these options are beyond the conventional "asset classes," and thus invisible to the conventional economist and money manager.

I hope to open new vistas on low-risk, high return investments of human, social and financial capital.

9 | The Spectrum of Risk

We have already examined systemic risks in the global financial system. There are other types of risk in local or decentralized investments. Our job as entrepreneurial investors is to assess the relative mix of risks present in each investment option and then choose the lower risk options that offer a high probability of outsized returns and avoid those which offer the probability of low returns while exposing us to high costs and systemic risk.

The difference between assets sunk into the global financial system and local assets you control can be illustrated by the difference between owning shares in an overseas gold mine via stock, an exchange-traded fund or a mutual fund, and owning physical gold coins. The mining company can be expropriated by a new government, and the investment lost. Gold coins can be stolen, and gold coins held in a bank safety deposit box could be confiscated by our government if "gold hoarding" was outlawed, as occurred in 1933.

Governments tend to confiscate what is easy to confiscate, i.e. those assets or revenues that are controlled by a centralized authority. Thus the government can rather easily order banks to open all private security deposit boxes and remove any gold coins, just as it can rather easily impose new withholding taxes on employers. Conducting house-to-house searches for gold coins is a far more costly method of confiscation, and the return on the government's "investment" of labor is significantly lower than centralized confiscation or taxation.

I am not suggesting the Federal government is planning to confiscate all private gold—though it has done so before in a "state of emergency." I am only trying to illustrate the different types of risk in specific investments. It is prudent to differentiate between risks we can mitigate ourselves and those that are completely outside our control.

Risk is ever-present and cannot be massaged out of existence; it can only be hedged by judicious choice of investments and diversification within all three forms of capital: human, social and financial.

A third concept is the value of control. As I noted in *Survival+,* the value of control is poorly understood, difficult to quantify and thus is not efficiently priced into markets. In our gold example, the mining shares reflect the value of the gold in the ground beneath the mine, the mine's annual production, the current price of gold, and so on, but all of these calculations of value and risk are rendered meaningless the moment the local government expropriates the mine.

The gold coins in your possession are priced exactly the same as those in the bank safety deposit box, but there is a difference: yours are vulnerable to theft from a burglar, while those in the bank are vulnerable to theft by the government. You can control the risk of theft from your home to some degree, but you cannot control the Federal government's confiscation of the coins in the bank.

Let's say an investor owns an oil well and thus has complete claim over the income stream derived from the well's production of oil. Another investor owns an equivalent dollar amount of shares in a global oil company. Both will be directly affected by the price of oil, but there are differences in the risks posed by each investment. The global oil company derives a substantial share of its income from "downstream" sources such as refining and petrochemicals, which continue to earn a return even if the price of crude oil drops.

But owning shares in the global financial system exposes the investor to market risks such as markets being closed during emergencies, capital controls, "windfall taxes," etc. The investor who owns the actual well can limit or stop production if conditions warrant saving the oil for better pricing later. Though he is directly influenced by a market that is outside his control—the price of oil on the global market— he retains some control over his investment.

The U.S. government could seize control of his oil well, of course, or arbitrarily set the price of oil far below market price, or place a "windfall tax" on the income; there is no limit on what the government might do in a "state of emergency," contrived or otherwise. Risk is ever-present on many levels. But until the moment that the government expropriates the well, then direct ownership still confers some control to the owner which does not exist for the investor in the global financial system.

Valuation and Risk

There are many ways to reckon the value of a house—its replacement cost, for example--but the functional value of the house is as shelter, and what those in the market for shelter will trade or pay to rent or buy it.

In places where there is a great disparity between the number of people seeking shelter (and able to pay for it) and the supply of empty houses, then the value of a house can drop to zero. We see this in abandoned farm areas and in urban zones which have lost most of their population.

In the early days of California Gold Rush, a single egg fetched a very pretty price in gold, as eggs were scarce and gold relatively abundant. The relative value of the egg was high in relation to the value of gold.

In the boom years, shopping malls in distant exurbs far from jobs and other amenities had great value because they generated income and had high occupancy rates. Once the housing bubble burst, then occupancy rates in these marginal commercial properties soared, and their value plummeted, in some cases to zero.

The value of a wind turbine will fluctuate with the value of the electricity it produces.

The value of an orchard will fluctuate with the yield of its trees, the price fetched by its fruit, the cost of borrowing money, inflation and other factors.

What do these examples share? Clearly, houses, windmills, shopping malls and orchards all have some intrinsic value, as they each provide functional utility. But supply and demand and macroeconomic factors such as inflation and the cost of money will dramatically influence their market value and the value of the income stream they generate.

These factors make up the risk profile of any object whose value is based on its functional utility.

Investors look at any potential investment as a claim on an income stream. From this view, the value of a house or shopping mall is derived from the rent that can be collected from tenants, and the value of the orchard is based on the amount of fruit harvested and the price per pound it fetches.

When demand crashes, then the value of things which have intrinsic value can fall precipitously. They "shouldn't" be this cheap, but if money is dear, cash is scarce and the supply overwhelms diminished demand, then the number of buyers willing to buy the asset will be so small that the price can drop to near-zero.

Houses can drop to zero value, and fruit can be left to rot on the ground because its wholesale price is lower than the cost of harvesting it.

The higher the carrying costs of the asset, the higher the risk of going bust if supply exceeds demand or demand plummets. If an investor borrowed a lot of money at a hefty rate of interest to buy a shopping mall, and the property taxes on the property are high, then even a modest decline in occupancy might push the property into a monthly loss, i.e. the monthly carrying costs exceed the income derived from rent.

The carrying costs of any asset and the reliability of its income stream are thus key factors of risk.

Debt raises the carrying costs, and thus it increases the risk of default or unprofitability. Some observers who anticipate hyperinflation reckon that debt will be wiped out in the hyperinflationary black hole, but nobody knows when such an event will occur. Those who own the debt tend to have significant political power, and thus they may get the rules rewritten to protect their interests.

The carrying costs of productive assets owned free and clear are limited to taxes and maintenance. The Status Quo heavily incentivizes debt via tax deductions for interest, but debt cedes a level of control to others and raises the risk to the debtor. Put another way: it's hard for bad things to happen when you have no debt.

Another kind of risk arises from the functional differences between various locally owned assets. Some provide what I term the FEW essentials—food, energy and water—and the other necessity of life, shelter. A shopping mall offers diversion and entertainment, something that humans value because of their innate desire for novelty, but it is not essential in the same way as food, energy and water.

A house offers shelter, but if everyone has moved away from the locale and sources of income are scarce, then the house has little functional value. Abandoned farm houses are a common sight in the U.S., and they reflect a long migration from rural farms to cities. Now de-industrialized cities have been losing residents, and abandoned urban neighborhoods are becoming common.

Electricity that can be delivered into the grid to many users is unlikely to fall to zero value, as the cost of generating electricity is non-zero and the demand is relatively inelastic.

As stock market investors know, the value of an enterprise depends not just on the profits it generates but what others are willing to pay for that revenue stream, and that calculation depends on the yields of other alternative investments. If interest rates are high and a saver can get a 7% yield on surplus capital in a savings account, then a bond yielding 3% or a stock with no dividend and a price-earnings ratio of 20 and an effective yield of 5% (that is, $100 of the stock buys annual earnings of $5) will be unattractive. Over time, the bond and the stock will decline in price until their yield is comparable to that earned by savings..

Assessing risk and pricing assets is not easy, and that's why it is appealing to let professional money managers make the calculations and let the global financial marketplace price everything under the sun. But as I have attempted to describe, the global financial market is riddled with its own intrinsic risks and it is inefficient in pricing many other risks.

In summary: risk is ever-present, and is present in many forms. The key difference between locally controlled assets and capital sunk into the global financial market is that we control or influence at least some of the risks in local assets, while our control of the risks in global financial market are either illusory (for example, "diversification" among assets that are tightly correlated) or extremely limited. The shares in an overseas mining company, for example, will be reduced to a curiosity if the mine is nationalized or expropriated for "the benefit of the people."

There is an "opportunity cost" to each investment: where else could we have invested our capital? The only way to choose wisely is to draw up a profile of risk and the reliability of the potential return and future value.

True diversification means spreading capital across all three forms of capital (human, social and financial) and across asset classes which we control, i.e. is outside the global financial market.

Risks of Globalization

Many financial analysts, noting the structural weakness of the over-indebted, over-leveraged developed world, have responded by advising their clients to invest in the developing world as a way to capture the strong growth and profits currently being generated in these markets.

If the globalization, centralization and financialization trends of the past decades are reversing, this reliance on the developing world for outperformance is extremely risky and potentially ill-advised. These countertrends are part of what I term the Four Ds: deglobalization, delegitimization, definancialization and destabilization, all aspects of a profound loss of trust in centralized global markets and the Elites who control them.

In broad brush, investors (that is, speculators) are "paid" to take on risk. The question then becomes: is the "pay" high enough to justify the risk?

Those advising clients to invest in developing-world markets are making some very big implicit assumptions, all of which are questionable. One is that the trend toward integration of global markets is unstoppable and permanent. In other words, that it will remain incredibly easy to buy assets and shares in any global market from any other country in any currency.

Another is that the "globalization is good for everyone" story will continue to be widely accepted as self-evident, and that the demand for capital from the developed world will remain insatiable in the developing world.

A strong case can be made that the forces of globalization are increasingly encountering blowback, and that the trend is reversing to local political control of assets and capital. The reason is straightforward: though globalization is "sold" as creating wealth for the residents of developing countries (a.k.a. "natives") and "lower-cost goods" for developed-nation consumers, the real dynamic is arbitraging lower cost labor and cheap capital to exploit labor and maximize profits from resource extraction.

In effect, capital is "printed" in the U.S. via fractional lending based on a tiny foundation of actual capital, and then traded overseas as the reserve currency (the U.S. dollar) for real goods and resources. The "natives" and the exploited nations are left holding a rapidly depreciating currency while the U.S. importers can sell the goods and resources into the global market for immense profits, which can then be plowed into further exploitation of global wage and resource arbitrage.

Even more perniciously, this flood of "free money" dollars unleashes vast forces of inflation within the developing nations, further impoverishing the already exploited "natives."

Trade in itself is not exploitive, but that does not mean trade cannot be exploitive. The difference is in the powers of coercion offered by the unlimited paper-money capital of the developed nations and the dearth of alternative opportunities for local labor. The other difference is revealed by asking, "Who owns the resources being sold for dollars?" All too often, the answer is a kleptocracy or small local Elite, who then transfers the wealth of their nation to their private Swiss bank accounts.

This structural exploitation leads to political instability, and an increasing likelihood that the kleptocratic autocracies will be replaced by governments that seek to conserve their nation's dwindling resources via expropriation of foreign-owned resources and by strictly controlling capital flows in and out of their country.

The conventional economic view is that capital flowing from the developed world into the developing world is a great boon for the "natives." This is an essential component of the "globalization is good for everyone" belief system. It is based on the idea that the key weakness in the developing world is a lack of capital and expertise, both of which can readily be supplied by the developed world.

But the same forces of centralization and financialization that have distorted the American economy and increased the disparity of wealth and income in America are also "exported" in globalization. These wreak havoc on weak institutions and populations without resources to counter the tremendous concentrations of capital and political influence that centralization and financialization bring to bear on small, underdeveloped economies.

While globalization greatly enriches the wealth of the Elites controlling the developing nations' income streams and assets, and benefits the small professional class of managers and government factotums, it often leaves the rest of the populace unable to afford life in their own country: inflation ramps up, traditional networks of supply are disrupted and replaced by corporate global supply chains, and subsistence now requires cash earned in a factory owned by local Elites and/or foreign corporations.

While apologists for globalization often point to the consumerist signs of "new wealth" such as televisions and motorbikes as evidence that global flows of capital greatly benefit the "natives," this veneer of wealth often masks a deeper and less beneficial layer of exploitation: land (or development rights if outright ownership of land is restricted) has been transferred to foreign owners and their local Elite partners, profit margins earned by locally owned manufacturers to the global supply chain dwindle to near-zero as the benefits of global arbitrage of wages, resources and capital are brought to bear by global corporations, and the financialization of the once-local economy by global banks leads to widespread debt which further impoverishes the non-Elites.

To bring the reality down to a household level: the subsistence farmer is encouraged to sell his seaside land (or the development rights) for the equivalent of a few motorbikes and television sets. Given our natural propensity for exploiting windfalls, this makes perfect sense. To expect a poorly educated farmer with little previous exposure to foreign capital to possess sufficient understanding and data to reject such an offer is to misunderstand the attraction of instant wealth. We in the U.S. witnessed friends and neighbors join the housing bubble frenzy as people who had an order of magnitude greater knowledge of financial matters than the poor farmer fell for the same financialization game.

In a similar fashion, the farmer's land presents an irresistible windfall to the local Elites and global corporations, so without any political or financial restraint, they will seek to exploit that windfall.

The global corporation then digs up the land and puts in shrimp farms, liberally using antibiotics and chemicals to boost the short-term harvests. A few years later, the ponds are too poisoned to sustain production, and they're abandoned, stagnant pits of weirdly colored water that are left as eyesores because there is no local institution powerful enough to make the global corporation remedy the environmental damage, and no source of local capital to pay for the costly reclamation.

In his brief period of wealth, the farmer borrowed money from the local subsidiary of a global bank—once again, a Third World corollary of the First World housing bubble—to fund land purchases at highly inflated prices, a natural result of the development wave washing over the local economy. Once the resources were extracted and the shrimp production fell, these waves receded—recall that the key component of global capital is mobility--leaving the farmer with big debts to global banks and land that had plummeted in value.

Lest we reckon the farmer uniquely foolish, this is the same story which played out in Ireland, Portugal, and many areas of the U.S. as the credit-housing bubble waxed and waned.

The farmer, unable to service his high-interest debt, loses the land he'd bought intending to ride the never-ending wave of higher prices for everything. Unfortunately, asset prices collapsed but the cost of living remains high. The motorbikes break down or are sold to pay living expenses, and the once-independent farmer is relegated to a tiny shack on a family member's plot of land where he and his wife watch TV all day long.

Lest you think this farfetched: I have seen this with my own eyes, as has anyone who has traveled in the developing world with an open mind and an interest in the local residents. There is nothing remotely ideological in the blowback against this cycle of exploitation, centralization and financialization: it is neither "liberal" nor "conservative," it is simply the only practical response left to the non-Elites populations.

Apologists for globalization insist that capital must be free to flow across borders without constraint, and that investment of this mobile developed-world capital (printed into existence) is always good for the local populations. But examples such as Japan in the 1950s and 60s disprove this thesis. Rather, Japan developed homegrown expertise and wealth precisely because it strictly limited foreign ownership and capital, and imported expertise rather than foreign capital. It relied on domestically generated surplus for its capital, even when the national income was low.

Meanwhile, the "resource curse"—the net result of globalization--has left nations with rich reserves of resources more impoverished than they were before globalization and financialization.

The world is truly interconnected, and so just as the exploitation of globalization and financialization is encountering resistance in the developed world, so too is it encountering blowback in the developing world.

Those who think buying an exchange-traded fund that owns resources in developing-world economies is a secure investment are missing the reversal of the globalization trend. The movements against autocracy and predatory Elites in the developing world will lead not just to greater democratization of the political process, but restrictions on foreign capital flows, ownership and the exploitation that flows from centralization and financialization.

Small locally owned and operated cooperatives growing coffee and the like do benefit from exposure to a global market, but only if they own the income stream and the assets.

Those who reckon China is the great success story of global capital and State centralization may find a restive population dismayed that the assets they reckoned would make them rich are worth less than their debts. It's the same story that plays out in every economy dominated by the centralization of capital and political power and the financialization of an economy without strong independent institutions: predation, exploitation, exponential growth of debt, reliance on opaque "shadow" systems of governance and finance, and rising inequality as global corporations and local Elites dominate the national income stream.

Before investing your own capital in developing world assets owned by Elites and/or global corporations, it would be prudent to find out the true dimensions of the risk you're being paid to take on, i.e. the potential for a complete loss of capital as blowback to globalization gathers momentum.

One of the themes of this book is that so-called diversification within the global financial system is illusory—it's all part of the same trade. When capital restrictions kick in, all your "shareholder rights" over assets 6,000 miles away will be meaningless. Trying to profit from an overextended system of global exploitation is significantly riskier than it is typically advertised, for it doesn't provide the diversification being advertised.

True diversification requires investing a full spectrum of capital (human, social and financial) into assets outside the centralized global financial system. The global financial markets can offer hedging opportunities, but the hedge should be significantly smaller than the capital being protected.

In addition to asking *cui bono*, to whose benefit, we might also ask: what risk are we being paid to take on? Is the risk transparent? Is the return worth it? What alternatives am I passing up to take on this risk?

Risks of Institutional Failure: the Super-Nova Model

Centralization was a key feature of the "factory model." Combined with mechanization and vertical integration, centralized industrialization and government enabled vast increases in efficiency and wealth in the industrial age. In the post-industrial era, centralization reached the point of marginal return: increasing centralization returned fewer benefits in efficiency while fixed costs of centralized bureaucracies soared.

All organizations can be profitably viewed as organisms: they inhabit a specific ecology, and go through a lifecycle of birth, growth, maturity, sclerosis and either death or transformation. The lifecycle of corporations is instructive. Enterprises grow rapidly if successful, and their fixed costs (bureaucracy) rise along with revenues.

But when revenues decline, fixed costs remain high. This mechanism is "the ratchet effect:" expansions of staff, reach and power are frictionless and exciting---the cog wheel of bureaucracy advances easily. But when the institution expands beyond its carrying capacity of its ecology, beyond the efficiencies reaped from advancing complexity and scale, i.e. to mission creep and sclerosis, then any reduction in staffing and fixed costs are resisted with the desperation of an organism fighting for its life.

As revenues decline and fixed costs remain stubbornly high, the enterprise loses money. Various expediencies and dodges are deployed to temporarily extend the company's lifeline, but as long as fixed costs do not fall at the same rate as revenues, the end result is insolvency once cash is depleted.

This lifecycle can bear an uncanny resemblance to the cycle of large stars that expand until their energy resources fall below a threshold. At that point their great mass falls inward and they implode in a super-nova explosion.

In the private sector, corporations often expand rapidly, bloat to great size, and then implode into bankruptcy when their revenue declines faster than they can shed fixed costs.

Since governments possess the power to raise taxes, their resistance to trimming fixed costs and declines in revenues is far more tenacious than any that can be offered by private-enterprise organizations. As revenue declines and pressure for real reform mounts, the embattled institutions find that propaganda and facsimiles of reform are far more expedient "solutions" than real reform. This is the key driver behind the flood of propaganda, bogus statistical "proof" of "recovery," and all the phony "reforms" laid out in thousands of pages of befuddling bureaucratic self-preservation.

Real reform would mean powerful constituencies would have to take real reductions in staffing, power, medical and pension benefits and in their share of the national income. Rather than reveal this double-bind-- reform is impossible but the Status Quo is unsustainable--the institution deploys its gargantuan resources to laying down a smoke-screen of bogus "reforms," distracting sideshows and ginned-up statistics to "prove" that the superficial simulacra of reform are "working."

But it's all deception. Nothing has truly been changed or reformed; another layer of self-preservation has been added to an already bloated defense of perquisites and power.

As noted earlier, the system's high fixed costs continue to increase due to "the ratchet effect" while revenues decline. A top-heavy, financialized monoculture economy that has become dependent on ever-greater Central Bank intervention and the "too big to fail" predatory banks is increasingly prone to what can be seen as ecological collapse.

America's centralized governmental institutions are all careening toward a super-nova end-state. They have increased in size to the point where their mass guarantees that once their energy source (as measured in fossil fuels and money) falls below a certain threshold, the institution will collapse inward on itself.

10 | Human and Social Capital

Economists recognize three forms of capital: human capital, one's skills, knowledge and experience that can generate income and value; social capital, one's contacts, alliances and networks which create reciprocal sources of added value, and financial capital which can be invested in income-producing enterprises. Financial capital is self-explanatory, but human and social capital are unfamiliar to many.

Human Capital

Human capital can be defined by what it is not: human capital generates all income which isn't generated by purely financial investments such as stocks, rental property, savings and bonds. In essence, human capital is expressed as productive work: the combination of skills, knowledge and experience that generates income and value from providing services and making goods.

The basic idea is that the more skills, knowledge and experience one possesses, the more human capital one has to leverage. The higher one's skill level, the higher the capital's value and potential income.

The spectrum of skills from low to extreme specialization reflects the risks and rewards of dependence on centralized infrastructures. This can be illustrated by a classroom game which was conducted by one of my high school teachers. The scenario was the classic desert island, and to start the game, each member of the class drew a "career card" from a hat which would define their skillset on the island. I can still recall the disgust of a classmate who drew "stockbroker." No offense is intended to stockbrokers, but the specialized skills of recommending and selling securities did not seem immediately useful on a desert island (the possibility of a lucrative trade in coconut futures did not occur to us).

As the economy devolves, all sorts of specialized skills based on "gatekeeper" certifications might lose their value in more decentralized, non-institutional settings. "Do the thing and you shall have the power," counseled Emerson, and that may well describe what skills will be valued as unsustainable centralized organizations implode: what you can actually do and make in the real world.

As with everything else, scarcity defines the tradable value of skills. Experienced doctors are scarce, and so the value of their labor is high. Manual labor can be done by the many people with low skills, and so it will continue to be valued accordingly. Leadership and the ability to work with others are always valued.

Many specialized jobs are totally dependent on institutions that are vulnerable to systemic devolution. The higher up a job is on the food chain, the more vulnerable it is to a collapse of the links below. For example, if someone's specialty is designing systems unique to high-rise office towers, and soaring energy and capital costs render high-rises unattractive, the specialized work will dry up. If that is the person's only skill, he or she will be left high and dry, an elevator designer on a figurative desert island.

Diversification of skills offers two discrete benefits in an environment of decentralization and devolution of unsustainable systems. Just as diversification lowers risk in financial investments, diversification of skills lowers the risk of dependence on a skill that could suddenly fall from demand as the system which created the demand devolves.

If we think of each skillset as a circle—a Venn Diagram—then we reach a new understanding of how diversified skills actually create highly valuable specializations. The person who has three overlapping skills in accounting, management and information technology (IT) has created a desirable specialty, as the number of people possessing skills in all three areas is considerably smaller than those who have one or two of the skills.

In other words, there are two kinds of niches—those which demand a very high-level skill with a limited number of applications (such as particle physics or orthopedic surgery) and those which demand a number of overlapping broad-based skills.

Every enterprise, public or private, requires the integration of finance, technology and people, so these three skillsets—accounting, information technology and management—are stable foundations of human capital. Since well-organized, professional people get more done in less time and can leverage creativity efficiently, then the fourth skillset of being organized adds a key component.

A person with these four kinds of human capital will be valuable to virtually any organization or network. Though their experience and skills are diverse, together they create a desirable specialization.

Over the past 60 years of ever-greater centralization of finance and power, it has been taken for granted that centralized governments and global corporations offered extremely stable employment. In other words, skills no longer mattered once you were hired; the security of the organization provided your security. Globalization and technology has changed that assumption within Corporate America. As corporations faced global competition, many were forced to eliminate entire levels of "middle management," and security has devolved from the organization back to the skills of the laborer.

That devolution is slowly spreading to government, as the Central States' promises have completely outstripped their economies' production of real value. Just as an insolvent household can maintain a façade of normalcy by borrowing unsecured debt for quite some time, so too are governments filling the yawning gap between their economies' production of surplus value and what the Central States collect and spend.

Government is only just beginning to feel pressure to downsize and become more efficient, and so we can anticipate the same process of eliminating middle layers of management within Federal, state and local governments.

From the long view, we can anticipate the continuation of trends which are already firmly in place: the continuing mechanization of labor that was once skilled, the development of new technologies that require new skillsets, and rising pressure on large organizations to reinvent themselves as sustainable entities or devolve/dissolve.

One way to look at these trends is to see them as signs that the long industrial-age trend toward ever-greater centralization has reversed as the efficiencies of centralization have now been replaced with inefficiencies, mission creep, loss of accountability and a fiefdom mentality focused on self-preservation.

In the long post-World War II period of prosperity, a college degree and a high level of specialization were scarce and thus well-rewarded. Now college education is common, and many areas of professional specialization such as law are increasingly oversupplied. There is even a glut of PhDs in many fields. We are constantly told that a better educated workforce is the basis of continued prosperity, but the reality is that many fields can only support a small cadre of highly specialized workers.

While some elements of globalization will reverse as nations increasingly choose to control their resources and capital flows, outsourcing of "portable" work will continue to pressure developed-world populations.

Another way to understand these profound changes in the valuation of labor is to see the entire post-war boom as dependent on abundant, cheap oil. As oil becomes increasingly scarce and thus more costly, then the surplus which could be used to fund inefficiency and misallocation of capital is drying up. The basic foundation of top-heavy centralized states and the consumer economy is eroding.

The other foundation of top-heavy centralized economies has been an ever-growing mountain of debt which has filled the widening gap between surplus (stagnant) and consumption (rising). Now that private and public debt has risen to unprecedented heights, that support is also crumbling.

We are in an era dominated by marginal return, where all the investments which once paid big dividends are now producing minimal or even negative returns as systemic costs rise. In the energy field, it now takes more capital to extract a barrel of oil or process shale into liquid oil, a dynamic measured by EROEI, energy returned on energy invested (or EROI, energy returned on investment, which to the degree that money is a measure of energy is the same thing).

In the realm of labor, the cost of a university education is rising far faster than inflation, even as the payoff from a standard degree is declining. The "dividend" from a degree that cost $120,000 might not even cover the interest costs of the loan that was taken to pay for the education.

This growing dependence on marginal return parallels markets which are increasingly dependent on a narrowing base of growth and profit. As the 1999-2000 dot-com bubble neared its climax, the incredible uptrend in the broad market indices was powered by a mere handful of big technology stocks. Once these few stocks reversed, the entire market collapsed.

The solution to dependence on centralization is diversification and decentralization, not just in investments but in allocations of human capital. Those households with diverse sources of income are inherently less vulnerable to downturns in any one industry or timeframe. Those individuals with diverse skills and interests are less vulnerable (i.e. more resilient) financially than those with one skill that is dependent on a centralized organization. Those with low-cost lifestyles are less vulnerable to disruptions in their income than those with high fixed costs. The same is true of enterprises and governments.

For example, a doctor who is able and willing to trade his or her services for goods from patients who don't have cash or insurance will establish a broader foundation of income than one who is entirely dependent on Medicare.

A focus on "gatekeeper" stamps of approval—degrees and certifications—might prove less valuable than real-world skills, as gatekeeper stamps are increasingly abundant and real-world skills potentially scarce. A reliance on "gatekeeper" certifications is a characteristic of bureaucracies and centralized organizations; decentralized organizations and self-organizing opt-in networks—what might be called the "open source" model of organizing capital and labor—rely more on what the participant can accomplish in the real world and less on gatekeeper stamps of approval. (The obvious exceptions are professional licenses to practice medicine, law, architecture, etc., as these carry the assurance that a test of specialized knowledge has been passed.)

As highly centralized organizations exceed their efficiencies and devolve to decentralized, open-source type networks, then the economic ecosystem will favor those with a spectrum of demonstrable skills over those with gatekeeper stamps of approval but fewer real-world skills.

Trust is an integral component of human capital; an untrustworthy person with high skills has much lower human capital than a trustworthy person with the same skills. Bureaucratic gatekeeper approval offers a formal certification of trust that can be used as capital within an organization that places a high value on certification. Outside of that organization, trust must be earned via results and verification of others.

For example, in the old centralized media, a single film reviewer could doom a movie with a poor review, for there were few sources of information about a new film. In the current era of decentralized, self-organizing media, a filmgoer can quickly aggregate a spectrum of professional reviews and viewer opinions. The "trust" in any one reviewer rests not on the position conferred by centralized media organization but on the filmgoer's own assessment of the reliability of a reviewer's past reviews.

Not all human capital investments serve the goal of generating income. For example, learning how to prepare healthy, tasty meals from real food is a skill that potentially pays enormous health benefits, even though it might never generate a dollar of income.

As health is priceless, then an investment of human capital in skills and knowledge that benefit one's health is extremely valuable.

The solution to marginal return is entrepreneurism, which is simply the shifting of human and financial resources out of lower productivity and into higher productivity. Ultimately, this is a form of self-expression,

just like martial arts and investing. Legendary musician Jerry ʻ
expressed this concept very succinctly, "You do not merely want ιυ ᴗ
considered just the best of the best. You want to be considered the only
one who does what you do."

For many people, being "the only one who does what you do" might
be a mix of paid work and independent services or production of goods.
This is a concept I term *hybrid work*, a mix of paid and unpaid, formal
and informal, largely decentralized work that is selected by an individual
to meet their goals, personality, needs and interests.

If we think of enterprise as a Venn Diagram, then one circle is an
individual's skills and interests which can be developed into skills,
another is what the community (locally or online) is currently expressing
demand for, and the third is what others haven't yet recognized or
visualized. These include the classic "unmet desires" and "solutions
which lessen someone's pain," where pain is defined as inefficiency, high
cost or burdensome processes. The entrepreneurial opportunity is the
overlap of those three circles.

Once again, control, diversification and decentralization are often
undervalued. Which do you consider more valuable: a $2,000 per month
paycheck from a centralized institution, or $1,000 per month income
stream generated by your own capital and labor? The average person
who still believes centralization is strength rather than vulnerability would
probably choose the paycheck, but I would pick the self-generated
income I control—or better yet, two or three such income streams, so if
any one dries up then my household will only be inconvenienced as
opposed to being impoverished.

As a reminder: reducing the household's base cost of living, its
transportation expenses and its debt load greatly diminishes its
vulnerability to instability and want. A high-cost lifestyle increases risk in
troubled times, as do single-source incomes that are vulnerable to "oops,
the rules just changed" realignments. It's hard for bad things to happen
when you have no debt, control several income streams and live close to
work.

The basic idea of diversification as an investment strategy--that it reduces risk and vulnerability to factors that are outside your control-- also applies to investing your human capital.

Lastly, imagination and courage are key traits of human capital, both of which are lost in institutions that punish risk-taking and independence and reward passivity, loyalty and obedience.

Hybrid Work

Hybrid work is a concept that should be of keen interest to the full spectrum of investors, from those with no financial capital hoping to channel their human capital into paid work to those with financial capital seeking to establish an investment income stream.

This topic is very broad and complex, and deserves a book of its own. In the context of our "spectrum of investments," it offers a fresh way of looking at work and the built environment which shapes our conceptions of work and investment.

The key concepts here are the same I reinforce throughout the book:

--Capital and income streams you control are more valuable than those over which you have little control.

--A range of assets and multiple income streams create low-risk resilience, while a "monoculture" dependence on one asset or income stream heightens risk and vulnerability,

--Invest in yourself and in the lives of others, not in Wall Street's global markets.

--This is an era of systemic instability, fueled by delegitimization, decentralization, deglobalization and definancialization. Relying on a monoculture concept of work is planning the future by peering into the rear view mirror at the rapidly receding landscape of the past.

In the conventional view, human and social capital is invested in a specific field of study or endeavor with the goal being fulltime, high-income, stable employment. For example, a young person attends law school (i.e. invests financial and human capital) and then uses his connections from university (social capital) to secure a high-paying position at a prestigious law firm. In a blue-collar example, a young person attends technical school and uses social connections to secure a lab technician job at a major hospital. In both cases, the employment is assumed to last a lifetime, though perhaps with a variety of employers.

That centralized, stable paradigm of work and human capital is crumbling, and is rapidly being replaced by a more dynamic model which is still so new that only the outlines can be discerned in June, 2011.

In the "end of work" era we are entering, conventional fulltime jobs will become increasingly scarce, and employment will become increasingly insecure even at institutions that were traditionally considered rock-solid such as government. Investing in a hybrid-work career offers another path forward for those who cannot secure stable fulltime employment or those who choose not to rely on that model.

My concept of hybrid work recognizes a vast spectrum of activity that counts as work, as opposed to the usual conception of "paid work," i.e. a narrow spectrum of labor that can be traded for money on the marketplace. Hybrid work recognizes value in all effort even as it recognizes the need to generate income via employment or via one's own enterprises and investments.

(The lower the household cost structure, the lower the income that must be earned. For more on this concept, consult Jacob Fisker's book *Early Retirement Extreme: A philosophical and practical guide to financial independence.*)

Implicit in hybrid work is the awareness that humans are not robots, and the need to have some control over ones' work and schedule is fundamental to well-being. Just as sitting down all day at a desk job increases the risk of heart attack by 50% because it is unnatural, stress is not so much the result of hard work as it is of work over which we have no control. One of the goals of hybrid work, then, is to seek work where you have some level of input or control. Sometimes the only way to achieve this is to fashion multiple sources of income so no one position becomes necessary enough that the worker surrenders all control to the employer, i.e. becomes a wage-slave.

Control enables integrity, choice, self-expression and the opportunity to put capital at risk to seek an outsized gain. The employee with no control is a wage-slave who can be exploited, coerced, deprived of dignity and devalued without recourse. The investor with no control is also open to exploitation and ruin without recourse.

Humans are "built" to favor variety and novelty, and this truth is also implicit in the hybrid model. Doing one task all day, every day, atrophies the human mind and soul. Doing a variety of tasks in a variety of settings is more rewarding and interesting.

The spectra of paid work and enterprise are extraordinarily wide, and so the opportunity for flexible work-lives and sources of income is also very broad. From the point of view of an investor holding a bit of all three kinds of capital—financial, human and social—then the goal is to invest that capital where it will earn not just the best return but the most control and the greatest diversity of income streams.

Put another way, if we invest our time and capital in a monoculture, we are being paid to absorb the risk that the monoculture will fail. As instability is the key feature of this era, then the return we earn for taking on that risk is completely mismatched by the stupendous risk that the Status Quo will not survive intact. As I have shown, if we follow the fundamental facts, the Status Quo cannot possibly survive in its current configuration. So betting your life and capital on a system that is guaranteed to fail is a poor gamble indeed.

For investors, hybrid work suggests that leveraging financial into an income stream you control is ultimately much less risky and far more gainful that compartmentalizing one's labor away from one's financial capital. In other words, the current paradigm compartmentalizes "work" into a monoculture "job" and monoculture "investments" into capital entrusted to Wall Street. In the hybrid work paradigm, one's work and one's financial capital are simply different points on one spectrum; thus "hybrid" refers not just a mix of work but also to a mix of labor (human capital), connections (social capital) and financial capital.

From this understanding, we see that each form of capital leverages the others; the whole is greater than the parts, as the three types of capital work synergistically.

In the conventional view, "work" requires accepting authority and centralized control of one's life. In the hybrid-work paradigm, dependence on top-down authority (i.e. work as following orders) and centralized control of one's capital (we'll gamble your money, you don't need to know how or where) are anathema because centralized, top-down institutions are precisely what is guaranteed to destabilize and devolve.

Hybrid work recognizes the value of Abraham Maslow's "hierarchy of needs" model, which suggests that various kinds of work address the fundamental spectrum of human needs, as well as our individual pathways to self-actualization, i.e. seeking our highest and best value as productive citizens. From this point of view, then some work is essential, and therefore it has unique dignity. Examples include raising and preparing food, disposing of waste, providing security and caring for children and the elderly. In our present era, this essential work is denigrated as "lowly," while financial fraud and sycophantic service of exploitive Elites is glorified. Needless to say, the Status Quo has it backward.

In the hierarchy of needs model of work, diversity of work adds unique value to our lives. In other words, a diversity of work is itself valuable, independent of the work performed. This is completely at odds with the "factory model" where individuals are cogs in a centralized, top-down machine, and the "value" is added by taking orders and specializing in one task for all of one's working life.

In hybrid work, one individual might have several jobs, each one of which serves a different basic human need: paid work on a co-op farm, where labor also confers partial "ownership" of the harvest, providing unpaid security to the community via patrols with other residents, some creative work that may or may not have a market value, and perhaps an investment in a local business that is in essence a fourth "job" in the sense that it is an income stream derived from investing in the lives of others (i.e. an investment of both financial and social capital).

In this view, Wall Street and its opaque playground of global stock markets is irrelevant. Security comes from control of income streams derived from social/human capital investments, not from financial investments in risky global strip-mining operations that use your capital to benefit a few at the top of the centralized-capital heap.

As another example, a physician might work at several clinics, having some managerial control or ownership in at least one, and also work as the unpaid physician in attendance at a boxing club for youth. (I based this example on the real life of a physician reader of oftwominds.com.).

In a variety of fields, job-sharing where two people share a single fulltime income, i.e. each works halftime, is increasingly viewed as a practical solution to widespread chronic unemployment. A number of physicians, for example, those with young children, have opted to work half-time, not as a sacrifice but as a benefit.

Hybrid work is not just a mix of types of work but of motivations and goals. That is, it is a hybrid of financial gain and social impact, what some call "social entrepreneurism." This model understands that technology and new models of work and enterprise can be scaled up to transform social and economic organization around the nation and the world at the local level.

Here is an example from Denmark that could be copied elsewhere and tailored to local conditions.

The problem was high prices and poor selection of organic vegetables in some urban areas. The organic farms are located outside the city limits, and the small farmer proprietors had neither the time nor tools to transport their goods to the city and market them directly to consumers.

A handful of tech-savvy young people came up with an opt-in, low-cost, web-based, open source, self-organizing solution.

The solution was a formally organized but collaboratively operated cooperative that arranges transport and distribution of the produce to its urban members on a weekly schedule. The enabling technology is a wiki, a collaborative website. Those city residents who want cheaper organic produce volunteer a few hours a month in whatever aspect of the operation they choose: managing the week's volunteers, helping load the produce at the farm and deliver it to the distribution point that week, divide up and bag the vegetables at the distribution point, staff the distribution to members, which occurs once a week at a site announced on the wiki site, and so on.

The distribution site is itself volunteered: a private garage, an unused warehouse, etc.

The wiki is in essence a database with a web interface. Members can select their volunteer time and duty online so everyone else can view what slots are still open.

While this operation is run entirely by volunteers, it is a model that could easily support a part-time coordinator who could be paid by a modest surcharge per pound of produce distributed. This model operates in parallel to the existing distribution network of wholesalers and supermarkets, but with two benefits: farmers earn a premium over the wholesale price and the consumers pay considerably less for their vegetables by trading a few hours of labor per month. It is highly decentralized and efficient, and the maintenance cost of the website-wiki is modest, given the scalability of the operation and the leverage created by the online collaboration and self-management.

There are no limits on the variety, flexibility or adaptability of hybrid work, which explicitly seeks to harvest the synergies created when human, social and financial investing leverage each other in decentralized, opt-in, self-organizing enterprises. As the above example illustrates, the hybrid work model is not limited to traditional narrow models such as "government-controlled," "global corporation" or "sole proprietor." That in itself makes hybrid work the appropriate model for an era of instability and change.

Settled Work and the Built Environment

Hybrid work implicitly seeks to integrate work, home and community, a synthesis that "the factory model" and cheap oil disrupted in favor of centralized, specialized work far from home—a complete compartmentalization of work and home.

Many jobs require daily travel (for example, those in the building trades must get to jobsites). Outside these fields, however, the easiest way to lower the household cost structure is to work close to home, or live close to work. Since transportation costs will likely rise significantly and long commutes take time away from other pursuits, figuring out how to move home and work close together is a key investment in your own time and household income. Recall that cutting expenses increases surplus income without having to generate more income. It is generally much easier to cut expenses than it is to generate more income.

This close integration of work and home was once standard practice in cities—my grandparents lived above their shop in Culver City, Calif.—but unfortunately, narrow ideas about urban planning and zoning have made such commons-sense arrangements difficult or even illegal in most American cities.

There is also a generational aspect to this compartmentalization of home and work. In the centralized "factory model" of employment, retirement means the surrender of productive work and the community of colleagues, and exile to a sterile home environment rich in distractions and "entertainments" but impoverished in terms of meaningful work.

The 1977 classic *A Pattern Language* by Christopher Alexander, Sara Ishikawa and Murray Silverstein contains an intriguing description of "settled work." Though the book is generally understood as a compendium of design patterns for architects and urban planners, it is more broadly speaking an investigation of how the built environment can be a permanent source of human well-being:

"What do we mean by 'settled work'? It is the work which unites all the threads of a person's life into one activity: the

activity becomes a complete and wholehearted extension of
the person behind it. It is a kind of work that one cannot
come to overnight; but only by gradual development. And it
is a kind of work that is so thoroughly a part of one's way of
life it most naturally occurs within or very near the home
when it is free to develop; the workplace and the home
gradually fuse and become one thing." (Pattern 156)

Alexander and his co-authors draw a clear line between the built
environment and settled work, and the process of aging:

"The experience of settled work is a prerequisite for peace
of mind in old age. Yet our society undermines this experience
by making a rift between working life and retirement, and
between workplace and home. The crisis of old age, life
integrity versus despair and cynicism, can only be solved by a
person engaged in some form of settled work."

Compare this conception of old age as a productive, fulfilling time
with the current conception of retirement being a forced reversion to
childish aimlessness and indulgence, as if TV, golf and finding some
excuse to get in the car and escape the boredom of life on a shelf is not
a surrender of vitality and purpose.

Hybrid work embodies the ideal of work encompassing a variety of
pursuits and duties in the home and in the surrounding community. Thus
"work" is not some labor performed in a distant place with no connection
to the home and community--the very essence of the "factory model"—
but a variety of purposeful activities built on the individual's experience
and interests and on the home and its surrounding community.

If we follow this idea back to the built environment—the fabric of
buildings, landscape, transport, public institutions and commerce—we
can see that built environments which encourage integrated live-work-
commerce synergies are worth more than "factory model" isolated,
compartmentalized concentrations of work, home and commerce. This
insight suggests a wealth of investment opportunities.

In a similar fashion, institutions and networks which encourage hybrid work/settled work will add value, while those that discourage it will decay. Entrepreneurs who grasp this will find many opportunities in helping institutions, communities and organizations become incubators of integrated enterprises.

These last two paragraphs could easily be expanded into an entire volume, as the primary idea opens up a vast array of enterprise: human and social capital are not isolated and compartmentalized from the built environment and public institutions. Capital will flow to the highest return and the lowest cost structure, and communities which encourage hybrid work, settled work and the reintegration of work, home and commerce will attract all three types of capital, while those who cling to the old centralized models will atrophy.

Social Capital

Social capital can also be defined by what it is not. If you arrive in a strange city where you know no one and have no contacts at all, you have no social capital.   Social capital is the sum of friends, contacts, alliances, group memberships and networks that create reciprocal sources of value. The key word here is reciprocal, as social capital is a two-way dynamic: it isn't created by entitlement or taking but by providing some value to others as well as deriving value from your association with them. Reciprocity is the heart of social capital.

Churches (by which I mean all houses of worship) have long offered a base of social capital, as they tend to be stable institutions of people who share similar values—one of which is helping other members whenever possible. Organizations focused on community or business associations are also often stable, as the shared goal of serving the community binds its members.

We all know the sources of social-capital contacts: friends from high school and university, family friends, current and former colleagues and clients, members of the chorus or band—the list is long. The basic idea is that networks provide resilience and a unique type of intelligence.

Neural networks might be viewed as models of human capital: a communication can be exchanged very quickly when various nodes or people are connected to one another, as opposed to a linear chain of command.

This network "intelligence" is the foundation of open-source enterprises, opt-in networks and self-organizing systems which grow and evolve by following a set of opt-in rules rather than by order of a centralized bureaucracy.

The value in human networks is that the person you know might not be able to help you, but someone else they know might.

As with every other human endeavor, there are no guarantees of success. Someone could join a dozen organizations and come up empty when seeking a job. Not all social networks are equal, though all have some value. The more capital (human, social and financial) held by others in the organization, the more valuable the potential contacts will be. This is why many feel that the value of elite universities is not so much the education but the contacts made with future "movers and shakers" and the offspring of influential people.

We tend to join groups which align with our own interests as opposed to consciously seeking organizations which might help us. There is room for all sorts of social capital investments, and the demographics of various groups are factors to consider. Those with older, successful people are more likely sources of mentoring than those with a younger demographic, while a group of young entrepreneurial spirits is more likely to be a source of entry-level jobs than a groups of mostly retired people.

Social capital is not just the value of various contacts, it is the opportunity to build a reputation for trustworthiness and a commitment to excellence, and to get valuable organizational skills. The vast majority of organizations depend on volunteer labor, and those in charge are keenly attuned to the dependability and commitment of volunteers. Those who fail to show up lose capital and those who show up as promised build capital. This may seem "obvious" but it is surprising how many volunteers consider performing reliably as optional and thus fail to build on the opportunity.

Many organizations are desperate for volunteers willing to serve as committee or event leaders. Providing leadership is invaluable practice in management and all the nuanced, complex skills included under the umbrella of "people skills."

Helping others builds social capital, doing a good job builds social capital, and being generous, gracious, polite and professional builds social capital. Everyone prefers to work with someone who is trustworthy, committed to excellence, generous, positive, gracious, polite and professional.

Online social networks do not have the stability of faith-based or community-based organizations, but they have the advantage of being global and low-cost. Many people have helped me over the years with suggestions for my website and books, and I have tried to be supportive of other writers whenever the opportunity arises.

Though much of what passes for "social media" is little more than endless "channel of me" self-absorption, i.e. a year-round "Christmas card" of self-indulgence and managing perceptions to boost self-importance, the potential social capital value of online networks has barely been tapped.

The potential for open source, opt-in self-organized Web networks to create value and open opportunities for individuals to participate and contribute is vast, and open-source software projects and aggregated resources such as Wikipedia are examples of what is possible by leveraging very little financial capital investment and abundant human capital into universally available social capital.

Social capital is too vast a subject to be covered here in depth; it covers an incredible variety of situations and networks and is extremely dynamic. The basic ideas are straightforward: the more people who know what you're seeking and what you have to offer, the more likely you'll be to meet someone who is willing to work with you. Trust is authenticated not by a centralized bureaucracy but by those who can vouch for your work and trustworthiness. The broad base of participants is the source of verification, not bureaucratic gatekeepers. The more people who have come to trust you to perform honestly and honorably as promised, the more opportunities will come your way. The more links of reciprocity you build, the broader your base of potentially helpful contacts.

Human groups are built on reciprocity and trust; that is the essence of social capital. The "mover and shaker" reached that level of influence not because he or she asked for a personal favor from everyone they met; they reached a position of influence there by serving a worthy community, by offering help and following through as promised.

Social capital has atrophied in many layers of our culture; "independence" and "security" now come from an entitlement check from the Central State rather than from human or social capital. This dependency on centralized authority breeds apathy towards reciprocity and encourages the resentful self-absorption of permanent adolescence. Human and social capital have been replaced by dependence on the Central State and collusion with a corrupt Status Quo. Yet this security is not as solid as most assume; the Central State itself will devolve as the financial system it depends on devolves.

As part of this atrophying, our culture and economy have become obsessed with amassing financial wealth that can then buy whatever it takes to be "comfortable." The presumption is that money can buy everything of value. But just as wealth cannot buy health once it has been lost, it also cannot buy friendship, loyalty, trust or security. Indeed, wealth becomes a target and source of insecurity rather than a bulwark of security. The servant can quickly become the master if the only factor is ownership of portable treasure. I would rather be in a ghetto where I am known and trusted than be a wealthy person cowering on my private island hoping my rifle-toting guards won't put a gun to my head and demand the combination to the safe.

I would rather have thirty people who care whether I live or die than thirty weapons or thirty diamonds.

For that is another characteristic of real social capital: it can't be bought, it can't be stolen and it is always in reserve for your hour of need.

A life without social capital is often a lonely one that lacks meaning. Freely chosen (opt-in) reciprocal relationships create meaning; giving creates meaning, taking does not. A person who retires with great financial wealth and little social capital and poor health is deeply impoverished.

Wealthy people tend to have social capital because their financial wealth was typically built on a pyramid of social capital. (There are of course exceptions to any generalization.) Yet social capital is not dependent on wealth; anyone can amass social capital, regardless of their starting point.

Meaning has value, though we have no metric to measure it as we have money to measure financial wealth. As the Status Quo devolves, we may see an evolution of what constitutes social status from owning the latest technological toys or fashion to various measures of non-material social capital. At the level of extreme wealth, this has long been the case, as wealthy benefactors have funded buildings for "naming rights," i.e. The Hildegard P. Stickslip Library, in exchange for the elevated social status such gifts confer. In response to rising wealth inequalities and material shortages, we may see a drift in what garners "perceived social status value" for the middle class "aspirants" who seek to mimic their wealthy peers. Owning an expensive vehicle, for example, might eventually be viewed not with envy but with the scorn reserved for the déclassé.

Most humans desire higher social status, as this improves one's chances for advantageous mating and wealth acquisition. At base, the promise of the consumer society was fundamentally a promise that higher social status was within reach of anyone with surplus savings or credit: in other words, status could be bought on credit. Human and social capital cannot be bought with a credit card. The consumerist promise based on resource exploitation and exponential expansion of credit will evaporate as the credit-dependent Status Quo devolves.

A revaluing of social capital at the expense of materialist measures of status would open up new avenues to "perceived social status value" and new fields for enterprise, just as the devolution of centralized organizations open new opportunities for amassing social capital in both traditional localized organizations and in Web-enabled open-source, opt-in, self-organizing networks.

11 | Health, the One True Wealth

Our primary asset receives plentiful lip-service but little action: our health. Once health is destroyed or lost, no amount of money or gold can restore it. Even love and admiration cannot restore health; former Beatle George Harrison, for example, was loved and admired, and possessed over $200 million in assets when he died at 57 years of age of smoking-related cancer. Health is truly priceless, yet few people truly focus on "investing" in their health by fashioning a healthy diet and fitness regime for themselves.

The general attitude is that health is a given, or that health is dealt out at birth and we have no control over what happens after that. Both of these assumptions are wrong. Health is earned, not given, and only a third of our longevity and overall health is dictated by heredity: two-thirds results from what we do every day.

Everyone wants more assets and income, but these measures of wealth lose meaning once you lose your health. The world is awash with wealthy people who have lost the ability to enjoy their wealth because they are beset by chronic diseases.

Our society's obsessive focus on that narrow bandwidth of financial capital is all the more remarkable when we consider the thousands of articles extolling the need to sock away several million dollars to fund a "comfortable" retirement. But what comfort is possible if health has been lost or degraded by chronic disease? There are thousands of articles on investing but few that connect the "investment" made in one's health to retirement and capital preservation. We are trained to obsess over gathering up $500,000 in financial assets while living in such a way that we need $500,000 of medical care to forestall early death from heart disease, diabesity, lifestyle-related cancers, etc. And the $500,000 spent to forestall death doesn't restore health; chronic diseases are not "fixable" with a "magic pill" or procedure. Health is the ultimate capital and the ultimate asset.

Modern medicine worked miracles when antibiotics and inoculations were found to counter bacteriological scourges of humanity: these microbe-caused diseases were effectively wiped out with a single compound that worked essentially identically within every human body.

But chronic diseases turn out not to have single causes, and so there are no "magic bullets" or procedures which eliminate them. Indeed, research keeps turning up deeper interconnected complexities within diseases such as diabetes and asthma.

What strikes even the casual observer of medical research is the number of populations in which heart disease, diabetes, cancer, etc. were unknown or rare prior to contact with Western culture and diet. These populations are in effect "control groups" for observing the consequences of the Western lifestyle.

A complete overview of lifestyle-related disease and a healthy lifestyle is beyond the scope of this book, but we can distill what is known down to a few key points:

The human species was selected over 200,000 years for the diverse diet and active lifestyle of the hunter-gatherer. Grain (carbohydrate) came to dominate our source of calories only as a result of large-scale agriculture that developed within the past 3,000 years—a mere moment in evolutionary terms. Thus it is no surprise that the modern sedentary lifestyle and modern diet heavy with once-rare foods such as simple carbohydrates, sugar and refined fats are poor fits for human physiology.

The common factor in populations that had low rates of chronic diseases such as heart disease, diabetes and cancer is that they ate unrefined and unprocessed foods and led an active lifestyle.

There is no mystery here, yet entire industries are based on debating exactly what constitutes a healthy diet. In general, a healthy lifestyle is based on eating real food in moderate quantities, avoiding highly processed food, smoking and excessive alcohol consumption, and living an active routine of daily exercise such as walking.

Such is the power of the food marketing machine and other cultural factors that remarkably few people seem able to consistently follow these basic guidelines.

Money is obviously a factor in maintaining health: it helps to have regular dental and health checkups, to live in places with good air and water quality, and to have access to unprocessed foods. But money is no substitute for a healthy lifestyle, and a healthy lifestyle requires rather modest amounts of money if you do your own cooking and devote time to exercise and fitness (a gym membership is not required to be fit).

It's not a healthy lifestyle that requires a fortune—it's managing chronic lifestyle-related diseases that require a fortune. While we cannot control our chances of contracting genetic-based diseases, we can heavily influence the probabilities of contracting lifestyle diseases. Researchers estimate that heredity only accounts for one-third of the causal factors affecting our overall health, and two-thirds comes from lifestyle—what we directly control.

Between having my health and having a million dollars (or equivalent), I would take health because the million dollars (or equivalent gold) cannot bring back health once it is lost.

Health is the bedrock of "human capital." The chronically ill person can have great resources of experience and knowledge, but these are greatly diminished in value by ill health.

Any investment strategy which doesn't focus first on maintaining and enhancing health and well-being (physical and psychological) is so narrowly focused that it is ultimately misguided.

In troubled times, a sound strategy seeks to shift reliance to assets we control, and lessen dependence on those we don't control. Since we control at least two-thirds of the factors that influence our health, then health should be high on our priority list of assets to value and nurture,

Once again, one size does not fit all; fashioning a healthy life is an "investment enterprise" unique to each individual. We can start with templates and guidelines, but the habits, routines and choices which ultimately make up our lifestyles are our own.

12 | Decentralized/Local Enterprises

I have explained why it is intrinsically risky to entrust your money to Wall Street's global markets, and introduced the alternatives of investing in income producing assets, in your health, skills and social capital, and in the lives of others. The next section covers the spectrum of investing options in local enterprise and productive assets. These investments can be financial (cash), labor (your time) or social (networking).

A central tenet of this book is that entrusting your money to Wall Street's global marketplace is a high-risk, low return gamble that could end with catastrophic losses. The lower risk, higher return alternative is to invest in decentralized, transparent local enterprises that generate income, either your own enterprise or those which nourish the local economy.

Global Corporate America's basic model is financialized strip-mining of local communities.

If there is one remarkably consistent characteristic of American communities, well-to-do and low income alike, it's that most of the non-tax money of the community flows to highly centralized, distant corporations. (At least some of the taxes collected return to the community in the form of government services, though these may be highly inefficient and of poor quality.) The mortgage payments flow to a handful of "too big to fail" banks, the grocery store is a chain supplied by global corporate food packagers, the "restaurants" are global fast-food corporations that buy most of their ingredients from distant corporate farms, the cable or dish TV and mobile phone subscriptions go to one or two global corporations, the auto payment is funneled to one of the global auto firms' finance arms, and the big-box retailers get their wares from China and other distant suppliers.

Poor communities are poor not just from low income; they are poor because most of the local income is diverted to centralized Elites. The money vanishes down a rat hole, never to be seen again.

It follows, then, that the first step in rebuilding wealth is to invest in local enterprises which divert some local income out of Corporate America's strip-mining operation and back into the local economy, where it offers a multiplier effect to other local enterprises.

As Wall Street is discredited and nation's financial and political institutions are delegitimized by their abject failure to protect the citizenry from financial predation, growth and the inspiration will flow not from globalized corporations and their political lackeys but from local enterprise and local entrepreneurs.

As noted above, I call these forces of blowback and trend reversal The Four Ds: deglobalization, delegitimization, definancialization and destabilization. Global predation and exploitation have ignited deglobalization, increasing concentrations of wealth and power have discredited the nation's institutions, igniting delegitimization, blowback to the financial system's institutionalization of fraud has ignited the fires of definancialization, and the Status Quo's financial and political over-reach has ignited destabilization.

A bet on globalization, corporate cartels and predatory financialization is taking on skyrocketing risk for dwindling, increasingly unstable returns.

The Grand Narrative of Global Corporate America

In broad brush, the narrative of Global Corporate America boils down to the endless search for higher revenues and maximizing profits, wherever they can be reaped and regardless of what must be done to reap them. This is the task corporate managers are hired to accomplish.

If you have any doubts about this, please write an essay on the following topic: Corporate America really, really cares about its employees. Hopefully you didn't hurt yourself by laughing too hard.

In the initial postwar era of 1946-1969, Corporate America prospered by responding to the growing market in the U.S. for consumer goods and for infrastructure in the countries devastated during World War II. As the

Third World colonies freed themselves from their colonial masters, then Corporate America sought footholds in rapidly growing post-colonial markets.

These developing world markets increased in importance as America suffered through stagflation and its consumer society matured in the late 1970s. Everyone above the poverty line had a telephone, television, automobile, etc., and as a result the consumerist society faced diminishing needs. To stimulate demand for marginal goods and services, marketing took central stage.

The key financial innovation of the 1970s was widespread credit, which enabled consumers to leverage their stagnant incomes into increased consumption. As stagflation eroded purchasing power—that is, wages did not keep pace with rising costs for housing and energy— then women joined the workforce in unprecedented numbers to boost household income. In effect, what one wage could support in the 1950s and 60s required two wages from the late 1970s and beyond. This decline in earnings powered the economic shift to the two-earner household.

The introduction of ever-cheaper computers and the Internet spurred a long-term advance in productivity in the 1980s and 1990s, a "growth story" that offset the maturing consumer economy. By the early 2000s, however, the tech boom had also matured, and consumer debt had reached the limits of solvency.

The Federal Reserve responded to this weakening by lowering interest rates and expanding the money supply, and the Congress cut taxes and financial oversight. This led to the financialization of the U.S. economy, inflating a credit bubble that infected the nation's housing market with widespread runaway speculation. As housing values doubled or even tripled in a few short years, credit exploded as homeowners refinanced or borrowed against their newfound equity to fund rampant consumption.

All speculative, credit-based bubbles burst, and the housing bubble was no exception. In the post-bubble aftermath, credit contracted and a fraud-based financial system veered toward collapse. Only extraordinary deployment of taxpayers' money and unprecedented expansions of credit and money supply staved off a reckoning.

But these actions did nothing to remedy the long-standing maturation of the consumer economy and the limits of the FIRE (finance, insurance and real estate) financialization of the U.S. economy, nor did they enable consumers to pay down their vast debts. Instead, the Federal government borrowed trillions of dollars annually to replace the lost private borrowing with Central State borrowing. This led to unprecedented fiscal imbalances which threaten the Federal government with an impossible fork in the road ahead: either inflate away the obligations of soaring debt, wiping out the nation's currency and savings, or default on its rising obligations.

Global U.S.-based corporations had responded to stagflation and the maturing of the consumer economy by shifting production overseas to lower costs and increase profit margins and ramping up sales in rapidly growing overseas markets. These trends gathered momentum in the 1990s as Brazil, Russia, India and China (the BRIC countries) opened their economies to outside investment.

As a result of these tidal forces, Global Corporate America now earns most of its revenues and profits overseas, and in response it has moved production and staffing overseas to serve these expanding markets. The U.S. is in effect a low-growth market encumbered by high cost structures, bloated government and multiple inefficiencies, and dominated by global corporate cartels that purchase government subsidies and protection from competition via lobbying and campaign contributions.

As food and energy costs rise and nation-states seek to reassert their control of local capital and resources. the era of centralized, long-supply-chain globalization is reversing. This suggests that decentralized, open-source, networked localized enterprises may outperform hierarchical, centralized global corporations.

The alternatives to investing in Wall Street's model of financialization and Corporate America's offshoring are many. I can only provide an overview in a book of this length, so the local exploration will be your journey.

The Value of Local Enterprises

Self-interest is a natural motivator, but it is not the only or even the prime motivation in human nature. We all yearn to be part of a larger purpose, an organization with an inspirational goal. We all yearn to be inspired, and to share in the success of a larger purpose.

An enterprise is simply a practical roadmap powered by an inspirational purpose. In the restaurant example I outline below—chosen because it's an enterprise most of us can relate to—the inspirational purpose is to serve and inspire the community with a fun and interesting place to gather and to enjoy healthy, tasty locally prepared food. To insure the enterprise's success, the founders and investors must reach out and help build a network that includes exciting community groups and fosters opportunities for other small enterprises to launch and prosper.

If we look at human history as a canvas of inspiration, we find (unsurprisingly) that both evil and good can be inspirational. Leaders can inspire with bloodlust, revenge and war, or they can inspire the construction of great art, great transport and great commerce. If we examine the great building projects of the ancient world, we find palaces to the glory of one ruler or royal dynasty are outnumbered by buildings inspired by religious devotion, a common purpose served by the construction. Examples include Stonehenge, Machu Picchu, the Parthenon, the Mayan pyramids and Egyptian temples.

Our era is dominated by the secular worship of one thin slice of human motivation: self-interest. We presume that making a fortune and gaining concentrated personal power is all that truly motivates anyone, and we pay people in order to buy their service to our self-interest. Lip service is paid to religious devotion and patriotism, but even these calls to higher duty are couched in terms of self-interest, i.e. what you're going to get out of the deal.

This myopic devotion to self-interest blinds us to the power and rewards of common purpose. The modern global corporation devotes considerable attention to creating a simulacrum of common purpose via human resource department's empty cheerleading. But participants know it is only a hollow, cynical ritual that everyone shuffles through in order to keep their jobs. The reality in the Global Corporation is that every employee is dispensable, and their position is inherently contingent. The purpose is to deliver profits to shareholders, and the corporation buys a facsimile of loyalty and presents a façade of purpose to keep the work environment from becoming overtly depressing to the human spirit. The reason they must play this game is the profits, of course; dispirited workers aren't very productive.

In a parallel fashion, the Global Corporation's restaurants—fast food outlets—are equally soulless, cookie-cutter plastic way stations where the food is exactly the same everywhere: unhealthy and bland. The orders come from on high, and are passed in military fashion down the chain of command to the employees, who are instructed with robotic rigor on what to say and when to say it. The supply chains bypass the local community entirely; the money flows elsewhere for everything but the low-paid labor.

If most of the earnings of the community are diverted to cartels and quasi-monopolies, then how much is left to filter down in the local community? The answer is obvious: very little.

In the fantasy version of capitalism beloved by Wall Street financial pundits and tenured economics professors, then the community exports goods or services to other nations to earn a profit on what it makes/does better than others in the global economy. But the reality is that exports comprise about 13.5% of the U.S. economy, and imports are about 17.5%. (The difference is our trade deficit, or current account deficit.) In this fantasy version, communities ship their local products to other parts of the U.S. where the products can't be made as cheaply. In theory, everyone prospers.

But the reality is there is little room in the supply chain dominated by centralized global capital. In worshipping price (low price is all that matters) and self-interest (the only thing that matters is that my self-interest is supposedly maximized by buying the cheapest goods), then we choose, consciously or unconsciously, hollowed-out communities which end up dependent on some form of Central State welfare, either corporate welfare or welfare to individuals, who are in essence paid to stay home and watch TV rather than make themselves useful in some enterprise.

As the Savior State becomes insolvent, this dependency on Central State largesse leaves communities extremely vulnerable to declining State spending. As many others have noted, the Central State has two choices: either inflate its way out of its impossible-to-pay obligations, or outright default. In the first case, State dependents will receive their $1,000 payment but will discover it now buys a single loaf of bread. In the second case, State dependents will find their payments have shrunk, been cut off or are only paid sporadically.

Any "third way" that proponents claim will enable the Central State to meet its $100 trillion obligations in currency with the purchasing power of today's dollar is illusory. "Taxing the rich," raising taxes in general, trimming the growth rates of fast-expanding programs—none of these will accomplish anything but delay the inevitable insolvency by some fleeting span of time.

Dependence on an insolvent Central State greatly increases vulnerability and risk.

The tasks left to the community are those where there is no substantial profit to be skimmed by Global Corporate America. These tasks are left to be filled by volunteers and threadbare non-profit non-governmental organizations (NGOs).

As investors, we have been brainwashed into seeing ourselves as disembodied zombies who float around the world, seeking higher returns wherever we might find them. We are disconnected from where we live, and are constantly told that our self-interest is only served by investing in fast-growing global corporations making money from goods and services generated elsewhere. Those who eschew investments in evil are mocked and derided; the only god for investors is maximizing profits, and how those profits are reaped and where they are reaped makes absolutely no difference.

This is how we end up with a glorified Colonial Plantation Economy.

Those who benefit from the current system have a well-oiled propaganda machine which extols the Status Quo of globalized "free trade" (free to whom?) and the financialized economy. If we remove our ideological blinders and calculate the actual benefits of "free trade," they turn out to be less stellar than advertised by those reaping the unprecedented profits.

"Free trade" boils down to a trade-off: in exchange for saving a few hundred dollars per household in cheaper, generally low-quality globally outsourced goods, the community of households loses most of its locally based economic ecosystem that supported many small enterprises and many locally sourced and controlled jobs. This interconnected ecosystem once collected millions of dollars that have been lost to the community as local earnings flow into a handful of globalized corporate oligarchies. The immense profits skimmed from the local community flow to corporate headquarters, where they are distributed to top managers and shareholders.

But since the top 5% of households collect 72% of corporate profits and bond income and the top 10% collect 93% of the nation's financial income, the immense profits skimmed from local communities do not flow back to the communities. They flow instead into the elite enclaves of those who own the vast majority of the nation's financial assets.

As investors, we are told that "free trade" benefits us as consumers and as investors, who can collect our share of the outsized profits by owning shares of the globalized corporations. But is the loss of entire economic ecosystems really compensated by a few hundred dollars in discounts on poorly made goods? No, it is not. The individual household's "gain" is trivial when compared to the erosion of employment, enterprise and resilience suffered by individuals and the community at large.

As investors, we receive a 2% dividend yield from the S&P 500, a rather paltry take of $1.6 trillion in annual corporate profits—a sum which represent a historical high of 13% profit margins. We also "own" the potential for outsized gains and for outsized losses. Those who benefit from your belief in the system will stress the gains, of course, while those studying the opacity of the risk factors will stress the potential for stupendous losses.

The issue here isn't simply "free trade;" most people recognize the benefits of global trade. The issue is what sort of economy we have when highly centralized oligarchies earn most of their vast profits overseas or from overseas production control most of the domestic economy and political machinery.

In this glorified Colonial Plantation Economy, the financial cartels skim immense profits from domestic debt-serfs who were promised "wealth building opportunities" if they borrowed gargantuan sums to attend college and buy a home, and retail oligarchies exploit consumers' obedience to the Prime Directive that "price is all that matters."

Given the meager 2% dividend, the opaque risks of overseas investments and dependence on overseas supply chains, as investors we have to ask: is investing in a stock market dominated by High Frequency Insider Trading and corporations whose loyalties (i.e. profits) lie outside our nation, state and community really that advantageous? Could we earn more than 2% without opaque, uncontrollable risk by investing here at home?

The Spectrum of Local Enterprise

As I have explained in depth, there is no way an individual investor can accurately assess the risks of the centralized global financial system, or its opaque markets dominated by insider trading, computerized High

Frequency Trading, cloaked Central State manipulation and a vast, lightly regulated shadow banking system. The rules governing these markets will suddenly change to maintain the Status Quo, and as globalization reverses then overseas assets will increasingly be expropriated or controlled to the benefit of nation-states.

The primary advantage of local productive assets you control is that the risks are intrinsically transparent and a reasonably accurate assessment of risk can be made.

As noted above, what we're "paid" for taking on extreme levels of risk in the global marketplace is a paltry 2% and the empty promise of capital gains. In an era of increasing volatility, 20% gains can vanish and turn into a 20% loss in a short period of time.

While the global markets offer opportunities for hedging and short-term entrepreneurial trades, local productive assets may offer higher, less volatile returns, while rebuilding the local economic ecosystem that has been strip-mined and colonized by global corporations.

As noted above, the majority of local earnings are captured by global corporate cartels and a minimum of 13% of all local revenues are skimmed and diverted to corporate insiders, managers and the thin upper crust who own the vast majority of the nation's financial wealth.

This is precisely the same model global corporations deploy in the developing world, where local earnings and resources are diverted into centralized hands and the wealth/profits flow to a handful of managers and owners. As an analogy, imagine a landscape where much of the rainfall is captured and diverted elsewhere. A once verdant and diverse ecosystem is starved into a semi-arid wasteland, unable to support the local population which has been transformed into passive recipients dependent on the "charity" of a centralized State.

On this basic level, local enterprise seeks to recapture some of that vast income stream for the local community.

A subset of local enterprises seeks to export its goods and services to other communities for an entrepreneurial gain (producing goods and services and selling them for a profit).

A third set seeks to leverage the Internet to market local goods and services both in the community, and where appropriate, to distant markets which are underserved or poorly served by the global corporate cartels.

13 | An Example of a Local Enterprise

Local investment often boils down to investing in a friend's enterprise, and unfortunately this is often a recipe for losing 100% of the capital invested. A typical example is a small group of people invest in a friend's new restaurant. I use this example because most of us can relate to restaurants as enterprises that requires human, social and financial investments. A risky, unlikely-to-succeed local investment shares these characteristics:

- The enterprise is emotionally appealing and exciting to the entrepreneur and investors-- "This is going to be a fun, vibrant place with great food," etc.—but it lacks a clearly defined, practical path to solvency and profit.
- The friend has limited experience in actually running a restaurant.
- The investors also lack direct experience in managing restaurants.
- Risk is concentrated as there are only 2-3 investors.
- There are many competing restaurants in the area already.
- The new restaurant offers little clear differentiation from its competitors.
- The entrepreneur takes on an expensive lease because of location, existing equipment, etc.
- The entrepreneur signs a long-term lease with inflexible, unfavorable conditions.
- Lacking firm budgets and realistic knowledge of startup costs, the permits, plans and construction run way over budget.
- There is no professional oversight or feedback at the decision-making level; the investors fear criticism will lead to the dissolution of friendships.
- The entrepreneur is inexperienced at launching and operating a new business, and has difficulty accepting feedback and

constructive criticism.

- There is no professional accounting, and the enterprise's true costs and losses are hidden in sloppy record-keeping.
- The entrepreneur is overwhelmed by the day-to-day operations of the enterprise and thus has limited time to network with the community.
- The entrepreneur has no political experience and thus no local political support.
- The entrepreneur's primary marketing tools are a static website and a few expensive advertisements. Ultimately, the business is counting on word-of-mouth for its success.
- The restaurant staff is made up of enthusiastic friends with little professional experience.

Regardless of the business, this is a recipe for insolvency and total loss of capital:

- An illiquid investment that cannot be sold easily; buyers are rare and fixed costs unlikely to be recovered.
- High initial investment costs and a high cost-basis of monthly expenses put the capital at high risk.
- Lack of managerial experience.
- No managerial system of oversight or feedback.
- Poor accounting and record-keeping.
- No differentiation from competitors.
- No marketing plan beyond the basics.
- No practical plan to construct the enterprise's unique role in the community or space.

Taking the same example, a new restaurant, here is a recipe for success:

- First and foremost, an entrepreneur and an investor group who is willing to walk away from the idea if the location, management and enterprise don't come together, i.e. the costs and risks are too high and the realistic return too low. This is the most important skill to possess: the ability to walk away from a situation with high costs and low odds of solvency. The key mantra: fail fast, fail small.

- Investors willing to be actively engaged in the success of the enterprise
- An inspirational purpose that motivates people to contribute and care.
- A practical roadmap to fulfill that inspirational purpose: we will serve our community and help build a self-reinforcing network of local enterprises which will put more of our community's money to work in our community.
- 10 investors putting up $9,000 each instead of three investors putting up $30,000 each. The number is not important; up to the point of impracticality, the more local investors who are involved, the larger the base of helpful boosters and talent recruiters/resources.
- The investors are represented by one investor who has no personal ties to the entrepreneur.
- That investor is an experienced entrepreneur.
- The investors provide a "kitchen cabinet" to advise the entrepreneur. The "cabinet" is made up of investors with professional managerial experience and deep community ties.
- The investors require the entrepreneur to meet with the "cabinet" or investor representative weekly.
- Lines of authority and legal limits on liability are codified in writing.
- The investors receive a small yield from the very start, for example, 5% per annum. This yield is built in as a fixed expense, just like the rent.
- The entrepreneur has experience managing a restaurant.
- A professional record-keeping system is put in place, and staff trained in its use.
- The staff is mostly drawn from the local community, and they receive training in professional conduct.

- All staff receives a defined cut of the month's revenues, not profits, as they cannot control the profit but they certainly influence the revenues.
- The entrepreneur and "cabinet" (or informal board of directors) keep looking until they find a property owner who is willing to take on some of the risk. For example, the first year's lease is very low, and future increases in the lease are stair-stepped to enable the business to grow. The lease amount is fixed and the term is flexible. The basic idea is to find a landlord who is willing to accept some of the initial first-year risk in return for higher rent over time as the enterprise prospers. Alternatively, in depressed areas, the investors buy a building outright and collect rent as their return/yield.
- The basic strategy is to seek out "partners" who have a stake in the enterprise's success: the landlord, local politicians, etc.
- The basic business plan is to keep initial costs and monthly cost basis to an absolute minimum, to lower risk and enable a profit margin from the start.
- The restaurant will be the only one in town or in a neighborhood. If there is a competitor, then a detailed plan to differentiate the new enterprise is worked out well in advance of opening.
- The food should be fresh, with a limited but varied menu that includes "healthy" alternatives and daily specials that draw upon local produce.
- The kitchen staff and entrepreneur design a "signature dish" and "signature dessert" which is difficult enough that few people would make it in their own kitchens but well-known enough to cater to local tastes.
- The entrepreneur and the investor "cabinet" lobby local politicians for permit fee waivers, etc., citing the value of the new enterprise to the community. The lobbying is low-key, professional, with the goal of building lines of communication and influence over time, as opposed to demanding a one-time break

with no follow-through.

- The marketing plan is detailed, multi-pronged and constructed in depth. The basic strategy is to make the restaurant a unique resource for the community and community groups, and to keep its offerings fresh and locally inspired.
- The plan is based on outreach to existing community members and groups, and on offering those groups a stake in the restaurant's success.

The marketing plan includes ideas such as these:

- Inviting a local politician to the restaurant opening.
- Routinely offer fundraisers to local charities, i.e. 10% of the day's revenues will be donated to the charity.
- Recruit the local artists guild to stage a monthly art show where local artists' work is displayed in the restaurant; a "gala event" is staged every month when a new show is installed.
- Offer special low rates for catering to local groups; invite small groups to meet at the restaurant and offer them special "group rates" on meals.
- Cater to local ethnicities by featuring special menus; invite someone with a local reputation as a good cook to teach the kitchen staff a favorite "home-style" recipe.
- Recruit local musicians to play live music at set times during the week, and offer them a specified cut of the revenues booked during their set.
- Offer community-engaging special deals, such as a free meal to those over 90 years of age, the local winners of school art contests, etc., and monthly "special deals" catering to large families, children, etc.
- Offer low-cost "loss leaders" such as $1 servings of ice cream.
  - Respond to food trends and fads with a unique version of the fad that draws upon some strength of the staff or community.

The outlines of a low-risk local investment are visible in this example.

Human, social and financial investments are understood and properly scaled to the enterprise. The proper combination of human and social capital is the critical ingredient; only when these forms of capital are available and the enterprise's inspirational purpose and practical roadmap are laid out is financial capital "paid" to accept risk.

Risk must be transparent and well understood, and then managed in a consistent, forward-looking manner. Standard business systems such as oversight, accurate record-keeping, management, seeking constructive feedback, etc. have to be in place. Marketing is not a layer tacked on to the business, it is the business. The enterprise must be in a unique space and actively seek differentiation and engagement in its community, be it a real-world locale or an online community. It must seek out stakeholders and offer them a stake in the enterprise's success. The investors are paid from Day One, but only in exchange for active (if limited) engagement in the enterprise. The investors, employees and the entrepreneur are the first stakeholders, and they seek to add new groups via an expanding network of people and groups who benefit in some way, however small, from the success of the enterprise.

There are many potential models for local enterprises: cooperatives and employee-owned enterprises, to name two. These alternatives to centralized corporate models of enterprise are flexible and adaptable to local conditions and needs.

As noted above, innovation is actually less risky than entering a field already crowded with competitors.

Here are two examples of such innovation within the food-service field. The innovations may appear modest but they have proven to be extremely successful.

In the first case, the innovation was combining a small ethnic market in an industrial area of low rents with an in-house takeout snack-food service. Customers who came to buy groceries could grab a quick snack at the counter and sit down to chat with others or simply enjoy a respite in their busy day. Since there was no table service, staffing costs were limited to the food preparers. All the snack food was authentic and freshly prepared.

This combining of ethnic staples at competitive prices with snack-light meal food service was enormously successful.

In the second example, a vendor who had gained success at local farmer's markets with her baked goods opened a small restaurant with a very limited menu and hours. The small storefront on a busy street is only open from 11 am to 2:30 pm, and it serves one main lunch item: batter-fried chicken sandwiches with a special jalapeno cole slaw topping. Homemade strawberry shortbread and a few other baked goods round out the entire menu. The small space is mostly devoted to ample food preparation staff, so the long line of waiting customers is served quickly. Diners who choose to eat on the premises use ironing boards as tables; there are no chairs or wait staff.

This establishment is extraordinarily successful, even though its chicken sandwich costs twice as much as a fast-food chicken sandwich.

These same tenets of innovation, quality and social capital can be applied to a vast spectrum of enterprise.

14 | Ecosystems of Local Enterprise

In 2011, it may seem that hierarchical centralized corporations with long integrated global supply chains are permanently ascendant. The changes described here—deglobalization, delegitimization, definancialization and destabilization—are long-term trends, and they will take many years to unfold.

In the long view, dependence on resources and labor that fall under the ultimate authority of distant nation-states greatly increases systemic vulnerability. Depletion of cheap oil means the costs of globalization will eventually exceed the benefits in many cases. As income is diverted to pay higher prices for food, energy and water—what I term the FEW resources—and costs of production rise along with energy, there will be less income available to service debt and discretionary consumption. As the promises made by politicians come due, taxes and the cost of borrowing will both rise as well.

Everything which depends on borrowed money or distant suppliers will become dear or scarce, and so local supplies of food, energy, water and other essentials will gain in value. The value added by centralization will decrease and the value generated by decentralized, open-source networks will increase.

Those goods and services which are closest to the FEW essentials will naturally attract the most interest, as demand for essentials is permanent, while those goods and services on the far edges of discretionary demand will be left scavenging for dwindling discretionary income in a field burdened by too many competitors.

The Networked, Decentralized "Workshop" Economy

As noted earlier, the centralized "factory" model has reached the point of marginal return. In many areas such as education, it is actively counter-productive. Top-down, hierarchical, centralized systems dependent on long supply chains—the equivalent of monocultures--are far more vulnerable to destabilization than decentralized networks, which are the equivalent of ecosystems. Centralized, top-down government bureaucracies are by their very nature insulated from accountability and thus prone to the same moral hazard as institutions insulated from risk. Lack of accountability is another way of saying that information is being lost or suppressed, which leads inevitably to systemic instability.

Locally controlled, decentralized enterprises form complex ecosystems that are parallel systems of investment and employment independent of the centralized, global cartels that have siphoned off much of the local economy's income and capital.

There is often a chicken-and-egg dilemma when the local economy has been strip-mined and all that is left is a big-box global corporation's "plantation store." Small green-grocers cannot exist without a produce wholesaler nearby, but if there are no green-grocers then there is no need for a produce wholesaler. Someone has to be the innovator, and show that there is a market for local enterprises that are alternatives to global cartels.

To many Americans, that a network of small, independent local enterprises could provide better pricing, better quality, better selection and better service, and provide a much more enjoyable and stimulating shopping experience than a big-box global cartel Plantation Store sounds impossible. But the "Chinatown" (more like Asiatown, as there are many other ethnicities other than Chinese) I frequent provides precisely these advantages:

The selection of goods and produce is broader, the prices are comparable or lower, the variety of shopping and dining is incomparably richer and more vibrant and fun, and the competition between dozens of merchants and restaurants keeps prices low and quality high.

The density of jobs in this few square blocks is extremely high, as are sales per square foot of space, and a vast ecosystem of suppliers, from wholesalers to family farms, are fed by this vibrant, high-sales district. The number of jobs created by this alternative to vapid big-box shopping is easily in the hundreds, if not thousands if the entire ecosystem is included.

This thriving, small-scale competition was once the standard distribution model. Given that 13% of global corporate cartels' revenues are pure profit and another significant percentage is overhead to support the grossly overpaid corporate bigwigs, a vast command-and-control structure and a costly Panzer division of crack tax attorneys to keep income taxes paid near-zero, then it's clear that the local Chinatown could easily beat the corporate cartel Plantation Store in price and service because a third of the corporate expenses are overhead needed by a massive, costly hierarchy and 13% profit margins demanded by Wall Street and the Elite owners.

In other words, the "efficiency" of global cartels is largely a myth. The Plantation Store's "edge" is not efficiency but exploitation of global wage arbitrage, access to cheap Wall Street financing, eliminating taxes and competition via capture of regulatory and legislative governance and a reliance on cheap oil to fuel their global strip-mining operations. Take those factors away and the global cartel corporations are revealed as high-cost, uncompetitive sitting ducks awaiting slaughter by lower-cost local competitors.

Local residents lose twice when global cartels collect much of the local income and send it to centralized corporate headquarters, as a percentage of the profits are spent subverting democracy with lobbying and millions of dollars in campaign contributions to political factotums. Local residents lose not only control of their income streams but of their political rights as cartels sabotage democracy by capturing regulation and elected officials.

A key feature of local enterprise is that it retains and recycles local income in the community, rather than sending it to some distant and unaccountable corporate headquarters tasked with maximizing profits globally. Thus even if local earnings decline in troubled times, local enterprises can still thrive simply by taking some of the cartel's vast income stream and returning it to the community.

In the U.S., nodes of local industry are found in a number of regional centers. These industries include polymers/plastics, avionics, biotech, battery technologies, software design, medical devices, analytical instruments, metal manufacturing, oil/gas development, chemicals, robotics, electronics and renewable energy technologies.

To the degree that these nodes are not fatally dependent on precarious global supply chains and are already part of a decentralized local ecosystem of suppliers, then they offer opportunities for local entrepreneurs and investors.

One way of understanding an ecosystem is to view it as an interdependent series of supply chains. One supplier can feed a series of smaller suppliers, which form a network that feeds other networks. Another way to understand a local ecosystem is to view each node as a workshop that produces a good or service. If you chart out all the nodes of the network, and draw lines to represent every transaction pathway (something bought or sold), then you end up with a map that looks completely different from the hierarchical global supply chain of the Plantation Store or Global Corporate factory.

There are a number of emerging factors which may create opportunity for local enterprises and investors as globalization and financialization devolve and oil becomes costly.

- Advances in robotics will increasingly lower the labor cost per unit of high-volume manufacturing to near-zero. As the periphery of developing nations with repressive, corrupt governance destabilizes, then the political stability offered by the core developed nations will gain a premium. High-tech manufacturing will increasingly return to politically stable nation-states as the value of low labor costs will be offset by the high risk of political instability. Owners of factories in destabilized nations will get a notice of expropriation as a dividend.
- Even fully robotic factories need a supporting ecosystem of enterprises to maintain the robots, retool the machine tools, code new software, and supply parts to the assembly. A factory that

looks devoid of workers actually supports a great many jobs if the supply chain is returned to the community.

- These same advances open up opportunities for high-tech "workshops" to compete with low-volume customized production runs by centralized firms. Workshops need not be low-tech; high-tech workshops have many real-world advantages over centralized "factories" of product development and production in terms of turnaround time, overhead costs and flexibility.

- Advances in so-called 3-D fabrication "printing" have enabled "workshops" to fabricate complex parts on the spot without any supply chain except for the commonly available raw materials: plastic, metals, etc.

- Highly integrated, vertical global supply chains that converge on a distant factory are exquisitely sensitive to disruption. Like all monocultures, they are dependent on a narrow set of domino-like conditions to thrive. If any of those conditions fail, production and the cost structure are both disrupted. As the global economy destabilizes, many of these vulnerable domino-like supply chains will be disrupted, opening up new opportunities for local suppliers to create an ecosystem of suppliers and a politically stable environment.

- Any enterprise burdened by a high-cost structure that is heavily dependent on cheap oil from afar is highly vulnerable to disruption.

- As oil becomes increasingly costly—the easy-to-get oil having been depleted—then all sorts of opportunities open up for local enterprises and communities. These include increasing natural gas supplies (if done according to best industry practices to protect the local environment and water supply), increasing production at low-volume oil wells, renewable energy such as geothermal and solar, and higher efficiency technologies throughout the entire economy.

- Many of these opportunities are not scale-sensitive and so they are open to local enterprises. Coal-fired electrical plants are centralized and high-cost, and do not scale down. Many renewable sources of energy work at any scale: 100 windmills built to open-source specifications spread over a community—a distributed model of generation and consumption--generate electricity just like 100 windmills in a corporate-controlled cluster. A distributed model has the great advantage of low transmission loss: consuming the electricity near its source is far more efficient than "shipping" electricity great distances over lines.

■ A strong case can be made that half of the energy consumed in the U.S. is wasted in the sense that more efficient processes could yield the same results with half the energy consumption. As imported oil declines in volume and rises dramatically in cost, then a vast number of localized opportunities will arise to increase efficiency. Cheap oil (which I define as $100/barrel or less) has distorted the economy, and addressing those distortions will open up many new avenues for enterprise of all scales.

■ Cheap goods depend on cheap oil, and when cheap oil disappears, so will cheap goods. Even as the labor costs per unit decline due to automation and robotics, the costs of energy and oil-dependent commodities such as plastics will increase dramatically. The disappearance of cheap goods will make repair and restoration financially viable choices again. This will open up many small niches for after-market parts manufacturing, fabrication of replacement components, and skilled repair technicians.

A complex machine is only as durable and reliable as its weakest part. If that part fails, the entire machine fails. At some point it will make financial sense to repair or replace that part rather than discard the entire machine in favor of a new cheap one.

■ As Bernard Rudofsky observed, "What we need is not a new

technology but a new way of living." What this means is that many innovations and opportunities arise from social and behavioral changes that are no-cost or low-cost.

Take improving health as an example. We already have an abundance of costly high-tech machinery, but any physician will tell you that the most important improvements to health are not a matter of new technology but of eating well and exercising regularly, that is, low-cost behavioral actions.

Here is another example. A community of wide boulevards and speeding vehicles is not conducive to bicycles. Were the community to cordon off narrow streets or one lane for bicycles only, then more residents would feel safe enough to try riding bikes. This increase in bike riders would then feed an ecosystem of bicycles retailer and repair shops, and encourage retail enterprises to relocate to heavily traveled bike routes. Soon, those retailers would become a 'destination," which would further encourage residents to ride bikes or walk to the cluster of "interesting" shops. The total cost of establishing bikes lanes is, in comparison to new highways or even repaving boulevards, near-zero, yet look at how much new enterprise this simple social action generates.

■ The book *Bowling Alone* revealed the loneliness and desolation implicit in the gadget-obsessed, "aspirational consumer," "looking out for Number One is all that counts" American culture. Re-establishing enjoyable community activities would not just be doing good, it's also potentially an enterprise for someone who likes that sort of work. For example, someone who sets up and manages social sports activities could make a living by charging participants a nominal $10 a month to participate. The $10 would be very reasonable, as it would buy access to team sports, schedules and after-game events at local pubs and restaurants. People need more than food and water to live; they need community, and a flurry of digital messages is no substitute for real activities and friendships.

- One byproduct of the factors discussed in Chapter One is that we are experiencing "Peak Government" as well as Peak Oil, Peak Soil, etc. Simply put, government promises of plump pensions and limitless medical care were artifacts of cheap oil and postwar demographics—both conditions that have changed forever. As a result, governments around the world have a stark choice: they can renege on their grandiose promises or they can inflate their way out of their debts and promises by paying everyone their $2,000 a month pensions and inflating their currency so gasoline is $500 a gallon and bread is $200 a loaf.

  The opportunity here is that small local enterprises can offer services which are no longer provided by government, or provided in such poor quality that they are effectively useless. Consider security, for example. In today's economy, a small business has a single option: hiring a security guard. That is simply too costly for most small enterprises, and so social alternatives will arise. For example, someone could coordinate do-it-yourself security within a neighborhood or business district for a nominal fee per month; everyone would volunteer a small number of hours so that a team of residents had "eyes on the street" at all times. "Eyes on the street" are the best deterrent to crime, and the community itself can provide this with a modest level of organization which could also be an enterprise.

- Government's critical role is to limit predation and exploitation of its citizenry and public lands by criminals or moneyed interests (Elites). Regulation is simply another aspect of law enforcement. The key factor in effective government is not the level of regulation as much as the cost-efficiency of the enforcement and of the other services provided. If a municipality and state collect high taxes but the roads are rutted, the schools dysfunctional and the security poor, then those are good reasons to relocate to a local jurisdiction which enforces its protective regulations while not overburdening enterprises, is accountable to its taxpayers and citizens, and which trains its employees to be courteous and responsive to its citizens. If no such jurisdiction can be found, then local enterprises need to wrest political control away from self-serving fiefdoms and local Elites and demand efficient, accountable local government.

- As local government revenues are slashed by the devolving financialized economy, then progressive governments and agencies will be seeking new technologies and practices to transform their low efficiency and productivity into radically higher efficiencies and productivity. This absolute need to revolutionize the delivery of local government services will offer opportunities to those who design and create these new systems and technologies. The old, bloated, unaccountable government fiefdoms will implode and be cleared away along with all the rest of the insolvent deadwood, and there will be an immediate need for new transparent, responsive, flexible efficient models.
- People want and need inspiration. Global cartels do not provide inspiration, as their self-serving nature is all too transparent in the unhappiness of their employees. Local enterprise can provide the inspiration and community that have been lost to corporate strip-mining and incompetent, self-serving government.
- New models of enterprise are now enabled by the World Wide Web: open source development of software tools, machinery (Open Source Ecology, for example) and education, for one example. These online communities are opt-in, self-organizing networks which offer new territories for enterprise that are completely independent of the dominant Cartel Corporatocracy and Central State.
- The field of education is ripe for innovation in the "workshop" collaborative model that leaps over the current hierarchical, high-cost, bureaucratic, self-serving centralized "factory" model. The

Coalition of Essential Schools is just one example of many new models for education. There will be abundant opportunities for employment, enterprise and social capital in education as the factory model is recognized as inadequate and unaffordable.

- The truly remarkable feature of the World Wide Web is that it enables both global trade and local enterprise. Here are two examples of this dual nature. Anyone who reads English can buy this book in Kindle format online, regardless of their physical location, for a low price compared to the cost of a physical book shipped from the U.S. That is global trade between individuals enabled by the Web. If a new restaurant opens in a community, online reviews by patrons on sites such as Yelp can generate traffic to the local, physical site—an entirely local phenomenon.

- Social media's real power is not in mining data to be sold to retailers or in advertising revenues, it's in enabling these kinds of globalized local enterprises. I have addressed this in my little book *Weblogs & New Media: Marketing in Crisis*.

- The Web has enabled small enterprises, localized and globalized alike, to purchase distributed Internet Technology (IT) infrastructure that is in many ways superior to the costly infrastructure of global corporations. Assembling an extremely powerful suite of business services is now a low-cost project that is available to almost any enterprise: free or open source software, low-cost data storage, low-cost subscription services, and so on.

The Web is not "free," as its servers and data centers consume vast quantities of electricity. It is also vulnerable to disruption at key points, a reality that recently cause the U.S. to identify any disruption of the Internet in the U.S. as an act of war.

Despite these costs and vulnerabilities, the Web has opened up tremendous new expanses for small, decentralized, local/global, distributed enterprises, both as providers and customers of these new services.

Interestingly, these new networks of IT providers and customers are establishing not just self-organizing online networks but more tangible networks in locales such as San Francisco, where some cafes now rent micro-offices and shared conference rooms upstairs to the entrepreneurial communities which meet informally in the café. This is an example of how enterprises in the real world can form ecosystems which feed off Web-enabled online enterprises and networks.

■ This self-organizing "cross-fertilization" of ideas and enterprises, both online and in in real-world nodes such as entrepreneur-centric cafes is a key engine of new innovations and experimentation. The low cost of Web technology and access offers new entrepreneurs and enterprises a key adaptive advantage: ideas and innovations can "fail small, fail fast" and be set aside in favor of better projects without major investments of time or capital. This cross-fertilization is a key form of social capital: the "cost" of meeting in a café with like-minded souls brimming with enthusiasm, ideas and experiences is a cup of coffee. Put another way, this cross-fertilization helps keep opportunity costs for new enterprises low.

These examples show that the spectrum of local investing options is vast indeed. This naturally raises the question for investors: How can we access these opportunities? The answer is localized, decentralized networks of venture capital and globalized/localized sources of loans for small enterprises.

Regional Stock Exchanges and Networks of Local Investors

The first stirrings of a movement to break Wall Street's grip on raising money for new enterprises by selling stock are now visible, as several states are exploring the idea of establishing state-specific stock markets. According to the Wall Street Journal, the Securities and Exchange

Commission regulations allow for local exchanges if the listed companies do most of their business in that state. Local stock exchanges would be a boon for small enterprises which cannot afford the high costs of listing on the Wall Street exchanges,

There has long been a robust system of private capital investing in start-up enterprises: venture capital (often called "vulture capital" by entrepreneurs with experience in funding from venture funds). While there are regulations governing formal venture funds and private investment (consult an experienced attorney before investing in private placements or funds), informal arrangements involving small sums are in another universe from Silicon Valley's Sand Hill Road venture firms.

Many communities have informal networks of entrepreneurs and investors, and interested parties can start connecting with these groups by pursuing the usual networking strategies and attending local business groups, local government community development meetings, tracking down enthusiastic start-ups, and so on.

All of this is a form of social capital, where trust is the basic currency. As with all things using trust as currency: trust, but verify.

Decentralized, Peer-to-Peer Lending

In one sense, giving your savings (surplus capital) to banks is paying them to do the work of finding low-risk places to "put your capital to work" earning interest. As we have seen, however, the banking system incentivizes managers to extend leverage and risk as a way of boosting their own share of the proceeds. This reliance on excessive risk and leverage in the service of self-enrichment is encouraged by moral hazard, i.e. there are no penalties for taking on massive amounts of risk and leverage, but there are potentially enormous private gains to be reaped by ramping up and masking risk.

Since the Federal Reserve has intervened to lower the yield on surplus capital (savings) to essentially zero, then your share of the banks' "skim" or profit from lending out your surplus capital has fallen to near-zero. In effect, the Federal Reserve has unilaterally siphoned off the interest that was once paid to depositors and given it to the banks.

This has encouraged investors to abandon traditional savings and put their money in various global "risk assets": stocks, bonds, commodities, etc. The Fed has thus incentivized excessive risk-taking not just in the banking sector but throughout the global economy.

Eventually, excessive risk leads to excessive losses.

This intervention on behalf of the bankers and the encouragement of systemic mispricing of risk and misallocation of capital has led to the development of alternatives outside the control of the central bank (the Fed) and the "too big to fail" banks. An informal alternative system for lending surplus capital has arisen to meet the needs of those who have been exploited by the Federal Reserve and the banking system: savers and small enterprises seeking capital to borrow.

Peer-to-Peer and micro-lending websites offer direct lending between lender and borrower, and new arrangements of privately placed mortgages and other debt are finding willing participants.

Trust is the fundamental glue of any financial arrangement. Loaning to an individual or enterprise introduces the risk that the person or business will not repay the principal and interest. In the banking system, this risk is supposedly spread out over a large number of borrowers. But as the global 2008 financial crisis revealed, systemic risk is actually higher than localized risk, and even more importantly, it is completely outside our control.

If you reckon a borrower is risky, then you can choose to not lend capital to him. If you entrust your capital to the banking sector, then you have no control over their risk management or how much of the proceeds will trickle down to you.

Is an enterprise trustworthy? Is a network trustworthy? In the pre-Web era, answering these questions required legwork and secondary sources. In the present era, the Web has enabled "crowdsourcing" as an alternative source of verification. Such sourcing can be gamed, of course, if the pool of sources is small enough, and the pool of sources has all the limitations of a self-selected group.

Compared to the purposeful opacity of the shadow banking system and a heavily manipulated global stock market, these intrinsic limitations on crowdsourcing transparency seem rather modest. At least with Web-enabled verification and transparency, we have a chance to verify, then trust, in a way we cannot pursue when we entrust our money to Wall Street.

Emerging peer-to-peer lending enterprises such as Prosper Marketplace Inc. and Lending Club Corp. pre-approve prospective borrowers, adding another layer of verification. These web-enabled networks completely bypass the hierarchical, centralized conventional banking system, and open new opportunities for small investors and small enterprises.

Abandoning the global banking sector entirely enables control of one's capital and risk management. This puts the risk and the work of risk management back on the investor, but then it also removes exposure to systemic risks and enables a much higher return on capital. The Web has enabled the emergence of decentralized, distributed alternatives to the highly concentrated conventional banking system.

Losses are always possible, risk is ever-present. As we have learned to our sorrow, the global financial system can only mask risk, it cannot massage it away. Rather than trust a broken system to manage our capital and risk, we can choose to control our capital, risk and return ourselves. As with so many other aspects of enterprise, the Web has enabled just this sort of fine-grained, decentralized, distributed, globalized/localized control of our financial and social capital.

For more on relocalizing the economy and local investing, please see the book Locavesting: The Revolution in Local Investing and How to Profit From It by Amy Cortese.

SECTION THREE
Investment Tools

Let's return to the primary challenges facing investors: if the central banks/States succeed in engineering inflation, how can we maintain our purchasing power? And if they fail to maintain stable inflation, then how do we survive the black holes of hyperinflation or systemic default?

One approach is to seek investment tools that can help us navigate the treacherous currents and squalls which increasingly characterize this era.

I promised a section for those whose capital is locked up in 401K and IRA retirement funds; this begins with Chapter Fifteen, Essential Tools of Trading and continues with Chapter Seventeen, Assessing Value with Relative Value/Performance. The following chapters describe three other key tools: assessing the value of local assets, hedging and diversification.

Chapter Sixteen covers tools for those with limited or no financial capital: Building Social and Human Capital. Just as health is true wealth, time is also our real wealth. As social capital becomes more important, then time invested in social capital can earn great and diversified returns.

If history is any guide, and of course it is at best an imperfect panoply of possibilities, there will be opportunities across the entire spectrum of investing. But we should keep in mind that the past 30 years saw the triumph of trends that are now reversing: financialization, exponential expansion of leverage and debt, and central bank/State manipulation of markets to suit the political and financial agendas of centralized Elites and cartels.

As a result, the investments and strategies which outperformed over the past three decades of financialization will implode or underperform in the coming era of deleveraging and decentralization. Bubbles inflated by leverage and financialization will not reflate, and we should look at what has been passed over as low value for low risk, outsized returns.

15 | Essential Tools of Trading

Risk assessment, relative performance, valuation of income streams, diversification and hedging are not just tools, but ways of understanding risk and value, and as such they are the foundation of investing.

As I have explained, global markets are intrinsically high-risk and should be avoided except for well-planned short-term trades to exploit mispriced risk and asymmetric valuation, and for selective hedging, i.e. capital preservation. Those with capital trapped in retirement accounts have few if any alternatives to investing in global markets, so the basic strategy in unstable times is to stay out of the market until assets "go on sale," i.e. their risk and value are both mispriced, hold those assets until they are fully valued and the risk is no longer low, then sell and slip back to the shelter of cash. This is the basic entrepreneurial strategy of moving capital from relatively overvalued assets to relatively undervalued assets, that is, buy low-risk investments and sell high-risk ones.

Boiled down to the essentials, there are three basic tools for identifying when to buy or sell an investment:

1) Identify a trend and ride that trend until it ends.
2) Identify mispriced risk.
3) Identify asymmetric valuation.

All the hundreds of technical indicators and quantitative techniques are directed at one of these goals, and all the great investment fortunes have been made following these three precepts. Indeed, the most striking characteristic of great traders' success is the simplicity of their approach. The great individual trading fortunes were not assembled via complex trading strategies executed on a daily basis but by identifying a trend and riding it until it ends or reverses, and buying into that trend when risk and valuation were both mispriced, i.e. "on sale."

A number of investors are confident that only physical gold and silver will hold their value in the troubled times ahead. For these investors, that simplifies investing down to one rule: buy and hold physical gold and silver.

My purpose here is not to debate that conclusion, but to offer tools for those investors who 1) need an income stream to conduct their daily life; 2) have a significant percentage of their financial assets locked up in 401K and IRA accounts that preclude owning physical gold except via proxy exchange-traded funds such as GLD and SLV; 3) prefer to diversify their assets, and 4) choose to trade various assets as a way of increasing the purchasing power of their capital.

As noted previously, I believe gold has a unique hedging value, a topic I will discuss further in the chapter on hedging. But gold does not generate income, and it has the unique risk characteristic of being a previous target of government expropriation; the U.S. government responded to last century's financial crisis by confiscating all privately held physical gold, and banning its private ownership. There is nothing to stop the U.S. government from repeating its 1933 confiscation of all private physical gold if such a confiscation is deemed "in the public interest" as defined by those at the national helm. We cannot be certain about future events, but we can assert with moderate certainty that what was considered "impossible" pre-financial crisis is entirely possible once the crisis threatens the political and financial stability of the Status Quo.

What is the probability of privately owned gold being confiscated, of hyperinflation, of a devaluation of the dollar or a default by the U.S. Treasury? The answer is of course that nobody knows; the risk cannot be assessed with any accuracy. We can make an informed assessment of possibilities, and of forces that would raise or lower the probabilities of these cataclysms, but this will remain intuitive rather than strictly quantitative.

Informed intuition has a place in risk assessment. The entire investment sphere is based on what I call "ambiguous expertise:" nobody knows what will happen tomorrow, much less ten years from now, and this can be readily verified by revisiting various forecasts by leading experts. For example, the consensus prior to World War I was that war had been rendered impossible by the many connections of commerce and civilization. Few if any predicted the collapse of the Soviet Union in 1989 a mere ten years before, and few if any predicted the rise and collapse of a global real estate bubble in 1999, a mere eight years before the mania topped and burst.

Thus all the financial forecasts, from a "muddle through" market lasting a decade to gold rising to $10,000 an ounce in a decade, are based on ambiguous expertise: nobody knows, and nobody can know. Humans' ability to predict the future is remarkably low, and deep knowledge and experience actually degrade predictive abilities, as "experts" tend to overestimate their skills and the predictability of the world. Amateurs have a more realistic humility and grasp of contingency and thus they produce more accurate forecasts.

All expertise in the financial sphere is ambiguous. As a result, we seek investment guidance not from forecasts but from trends and relationships between risk and value that we can measure and compare.

Why do values and risk change? The most basic answer is two-fold. Change, like time itself, is embedded in the nature of our universe, and so value and risk are responding to changes in reality. Secondly, human nature: being social animals, humans respond strongly to the "herd instinct", also known as group-think. When an asset class is in favor with the herd, that creates a positive feedback as more herd's positive sentiment drives the market higher, eventually drawing in the last skeptics who are vulnerable to group-think. This drives overvaluation and increases risk, as the asset class is "priced to perfection," that is, it is now valued as if every positive trend will continue rising.

Once the last skeptics have joined the herd, and the more speculative members of the herd have leveraged their assets to buy more at inflated prices, then the herd goes off the cliff as prices plummet. With no more buyers to push prices higher, then the first decline triggers margin calls on the overleveraged members, who must sell to preserve what's left of their capital. That wave of selling launches another positive feedback, this time to the downside. Only the lead animals in the herd can see the cliff approaching, and by that time the momentum of the herd behind them precludes veering away.

Once the broken bodies at the base of the cliff are cleared away, the asset class is discredited; the risk has been wrung out of it, and contrarian investors with an understanding of income streams and relative value start picking over the shattered remains. The asset class may be "on sale," if relative value and risk are both scraping the bottom of historic relationships with other assets and there is still an income stream being generated by the asset.

Professional traders and managers rely on technical analysis tools to help them identify these tops and bottoms in sentiment and valuation.

Since there is a wealth of technical analysis material (both online and in books) aimed at identifying trends and trend reversals, I am not going to address what is already more than adequately covered elsewhere. These technical tools boil down to measures of trend (such as moving averages), momentum (such as DMI and RSI), sentiment (such as the VIX, the so-called "fear index"), cyclicality (four-year cycle, etc.), patterns (pennants, megaphones, wave counts, etc.) and probability, which is often measured by "reversion to the mean" statistical tools such as standard deviation.

A veritable thicket of online and book-length elaborations of these basic technical-analysis tools are readily accessible, and so I would not be adding much value with yet another discussion. These tools offer enduring value, but they are not infallible, and the edge they provide is thinned by their ubiquity. In our forest analogy, every square inch of every market is covered by traders using some combination of these tools, and so precious little light filters down to the forest floor.

As noted previously, no system based on mechanical/programmable signals works forever, and if programming these techniques into a mechanical system were all that was required to generate 18 high-return hedged trades, then every technical trader would be a millionaire (in 2011 dollars) in short order. Yet very few make millions from mechanical trading of these techniques, and even fewer do so in the long haul over both Bull and Bear markets.

As a result, while acknowledging the value of these trend-identifying tools, I will focus on mispriced risk and asymmetric valuations as tools which offer insights that are easily lost in the crowded technical analysis field.

As you know by now, I favor simple analogies to complex explanations, and so I will launch our investigation of trading tools with a game of eight-ball (pool or billiards) analogy.

The object of eight-ball is to sink a set of seven balls (striped or solid color, one set to each player) into the pockets of the pool table. The game is won by directing the eight-ball into a pocket identified by the player before the shot is attempted (a "called pocket"). A player gets another turn every time he shoots a ball of his set into a pocket. If he fails to do so, then the other player gets the turn.

At the highest level of skill, players routinely make difficult shots, one after the other. In our analogy, this is akin to master traders picking one high-return winning trade after another.

Despite the low probabilities of success in attempting difficult "trick" shots, beginners routinely "invest" their turns in these high-risk, low-probability shots; when one actually falls their way, their satisfaction is immense. That satisfaction is the reward for taking on the risk. But that satisfaction required ten turns and thus the opportunity cost—the alternative choice that was given up—was giving up nine lower risk shots.

The amateur pursuing the high risk, difficult shot strategy will consistently lose the game to other amateurs with no higher skills but a much more successful low-risk, higher probability strategy.

The less experienced player is better served by a strategy of using each turn to set up an easy shot next turn—that is, to "invest" a turn in nudging a ball toward a pocket so it will be a high-probability shot next turn. It is emotionally appealing to attempt a trick shot, but pursuing that as a strategy leads to losing the game.

This strategy offers a model for investing: rather than invest in high-risk, low-return gambles that carry huge opportunity costs—that is, we could have invested that capital elsewhere at much lower risk and much higher return--we are better served by a strategy of patiently setting up a low-risk, high-probability investment.

The previous analogies of guerrilla investing and hunter-gatherer investing made the same point: seek out the low-risk, high-return investment with low opportunity costs, and pass on the high-risk, low-return gambles with high opportunity costs.

These implies a critical ability to avoid being drawn into herd behavior—following the consensus "pack" into high-risk, low returns investments because "everybody else is making huge profits in this."

Just as those in the middle of the herd cannot see the cliff edge just ahead, the well-fed turkey can be forgiven thinking that he is a pampered pet. It is only in the week before Thanksgiving that his misperception of risk is tragically corrected.

Perceived Risk and Real Risk

What's the difference between real risk and perceived risk?

In 2006, the real risks of the housing bubble imploding were rising by the month, as all credit-financial bubbles eventually burst. Many analysts saw the real risk was rising, but running-with-the-herd participants, unable to see the cliff edge, perceived the risk as low.

Today we have global markets in stocks, bonds and commodities that essentially trade together as one "risk trade." The perceived risk that all three markets could suffer precipitous declines is low, as participants believe that 1) central banks will never let stocks fall; 2) central banks will keep interest rates low indefinitely, so bonds will retain their value and 3) the rise of developing economies will drive permanently higher demand for commodities.

From the point of view established in the first chapters of this book, all these perceptions of low risk are deeply flawed; despite the apparent differences in each of these markets, the real risk in each is dramatically higher than the perceived risk.

Low perceived risk and high real risk is the worst of all possible investment worlds, as it combines high risk of capital loss and low return for taking on that high risk. Recall that investors are "paid" in relation to perceived risk: a low-risk investment has a low yield.

Consider the investment advice often offered to those holding 401K and IRA retirement accounts: don't risk trading in individual stocks, put your capital in index funds which match the returns of the broad market. In long-running Bull markets, for example 1982 to 1999, then this passive investing strategy yielded remarkable returns.

But in the secular Bear market of 2000 to 2010, "safe" index funds yielded losses of 40% (S&P 500 index funds). After adjusting for the loss of purchasing power (what most call "inflation" but which can also be seen as dollar depreciation), then passively holding an index fund from January 2000 to January 2010 was an investing catastrophe.

Index funds are as vulnerable to systemic market collapses and breakdowns as any equity. Thus index funds do not magically eliminate risk; they simply pool the risks of individual stocks.

Just as low perceived risk and high real risk is the worst of all possible investment worlds, high perceived risk and low real risk is the ideal setup for low-risk gains. Why is this so? Since investors are paid according to perceived risk, high perceived risk is compensated with high returns. For example, a bond issued by a company or nation at high risk of default will pay an extraordinarily high rate of yield to compensate investors for this high risk. (As I write in mid-2011, bonds issued by Greece are yielding 28%, compared to 2% for equivalent U.S. Treasury bonds.)

But what if your analysis finds that the actual risk of default is quite modest? If the market perceives the risk as high, then you will be paid handsomely to take on the risk of default. If the real risk is low, then you are earning an outsized return on the herd's mispricing of risk.

Assessing the risk of default is more art than science, for any number of reasons such as fraud, unexpected default by counterparties, political crisis and so on. But informed assessments occasionally offer value. For example, I followed a large publicly traded medical supply as its stock fell from $5 per share to under 20 cents per share; the company had taken on enormous debt loads to finance acquisitions and default was perceived as inevitable. An examination of the company's publicly posted balance sheets and profit-loss statements led me to conclude that the company's cash flow was so large and stable that default was unlikely. As a result, I bought a large number of shares at 17 cents and sold them a year later for $2.25 per share when the company was acquired. (Following litigation, a competing bid was accepted months later for $5 per share.)

Consider a small pharmaceutical company with several potential medications in development. (This example is based on real companies I have invested in.) One promising research effort fails to produce results at a critical juncture, and the company's stock collapses as sellers give up hope that the company can create value out of its intellectual property and staff expertise. In some cases, the value of the stock drops below the cash held by the company, i.e. its cash value.

At that point the risk of loss of capital is low, as the company could close and shareholders would realize a gain just from the cash in the bank being distributed. Since the company has several other projects in development, the investor armed with a bit of bioscience knowledge might conclude that the probability is relatively constructive that one project will pan out at some point. The yield from any gain in valuation would be quite high, given the negative valuation given to the company's research. In other words, the company's intellectual property and research is priced at less than zero, as the shares trade for less than the company's cash in the bank.

This is a classic asymmetry between perceived risk, which is high—in other words, the company is being priced by market participants as if bankruptcy is assured—and real risk, which is essentially zero in terms of capital loss over the short-term. This mispricing of risk creates a hugely asymmetric valuation.

Measures of market sentiment such as the VIX "fear index" (some traders prefer the VXO variant) can be used to identify mispriced risk. When the VIX shoots up above the upper Bollinger Band (or equivalent measure of high and low price range), then herd "fear" is high and market participants are buying put options as a hedge against further declines in the stock market. Many traders have noted that such excesses of fear correspond to market lows, and are thus "buy" signals. In other words, the perceived risk of further declines is high, but the extremes of negative sentiment measured by the VIX indicate the real risk of further decline is rather low. Put another way, risk has been wrung out of the market when perceived risk is high and real risk is low.

When the VIX dips below the lower Bollinger band, this indicates that perceived risk is low (complacency) and thus the real risk is high, as complacent markets are eventually "surprised" by unwelcome news. In market terminology, a low VIX reading means participants aren't paying much to hedge against declines. Traders have noted that market declines correspond to low VIX readings, so this extreme of complacent sentiment is a "sell" signal, just as an extreme of fear was a "buy" signal.

The trick, of course, is to separate oneself from the herd and make an independent assessment of perceived and real risk. Many times, the two align: the company priced for bankruptcy does go bankrupt, and the firm priced for continued high growth does indeed continue growing rapidly. Contrarianism is no guarantee in and of itself; the point here is to distinguish perceived risk (group-think), a product of the immensely influential herd, from often-ambiguous reality (real risk). In the two cases mentioned above, an acquaintance with financial and scientific facts provided the leverage needed to distinguish between perceived (herd) risk and real risk.

Even without such knowledge, the tools described below can help us make that assessment and distinction.

This distinction between perceived and real risk can be applied to all sorts of investments, for example a college education and the restaurant example described in Chapter Thirteen.

Borrowing $100,000 (in 2011 dollars) to earn a university degree with little prospect of increasing earnings over a much cheaper educational investment is a classic asymmetry of perceived and real risk. The herd sees the risk-return of a costly college degree as highly beneficial, based on past eras in which a college education was a scarce commodity, while the real risk of such a large debt and uncertain return increases the risk that the graduate will be reduced to a debt-serf.

Compare that to a university education obtained from a state university, funded by family savings and part-time work and a low-cost lifestyle, i.e. living at home or with a relative, brown-bag lunches, etc. in a field which offers some leverage in slack labor markets.

Restaurants are notoriously risky investments, as the entry costs are high and most fail within a few months or years. The perceived risk is high, and for good reason, especially in an era of declining disposable income. Yet in the right conditions, the real risk can be far lower: if entry costs are low and there is no debt, if there are no direct competitors, if the managers are experienced at controlling costs so breakeven is low, if the food is plentiful, fresh and tasty, and if the owners are adept at investing social capital in the community.

Once again, the goal is independence of the herd's perception and an ability to realistically assess real risk.

Diversification

I have discussed diversification as a key way of reducing risk and increasing resilience throughout the book. The basic idea is that spreading capital over assets which have low perceived risk and high real risk creates an illusion of diversification rather than real diversification. Even though the assets are quite different on the surface, if their risk profiles are the same then the diversification is only superficial.

In other words, diversification among assets that are tightly correlated in risk and trend is illusory.

Spreading assets over stocks, bonds and commodities in both global and domestic markets is a diversifying strategy that is supposed to lower risk. But to the degree these are facets of the same trade in an increasingly risky global system, they represent very little diversification. As I noted earlier, the governments' propping up of assets introduces moral hazard on a grand scale; this is one reason why all global markets move as one trade.

Another reason for this tight correlation is the central bank/Central State leaders around the world have no Plan B, so they continue pushing "extend and pretend" measures which ramp up risk in all the asset classes they're supporting. China, Japan and Germany do whatever is necessary to support their exports, the U.S., Europe, Japan and China all prop up their insolvent, incestuous banking sectors, central banks print money to suppress interest rates, fueling more moral hazard, and Central States borrow money to prop up the Status Quo. Given this global correlation of policy, there is little wonder all global markets are also correlated.

Trying to profit from an overextended system of global exploitation is significantly riskier than it is advertised, so it doesn't provide the promised diversification.

Given the rising risk in global markets, diversification must be viewed not just as a choice of asset classes, but as a choice between those assets you control (decentralized, local) and those you don't control (global, centralized).

Real diversification means putting all three types of capital (human, social and financial) to work across the entire spectrum of investments that are outside the centralized global financial system.

The basic idea of diversification as an investment strategy--that it reduces risk and vulnerability to factors that are outside your control-- also applies to investing your human and social capital. Diversification of skills offers two discrete benefits in an environment of decentralization and devolution of unsustainable systems. Just as diversification lowers risk in financial investments, diversification of skills lowers the risk of dependence on a skill that could suddenly fall out of demand.

Diversification and decentralization are two sides of the same coin, and both are undervalued in a centralized Status Quo. This goes back to my earlier question: which do you consider more valuable: a $2,000 per month paycheck from a centralized organization, or $1,000 per month income stream generated by your own capital? The person who still believes centralization is not vulnerability but strength would probably choose the paycheck, but the self-generated, decentralized income is the only one independent of centralized global markets and thus the only real diversification.

Direct control of income-producing assets is qualitatively different from owning assets in the global financial system. Thus real diversification—that is, distributing the risk of catastrophic loss over a number of assets--requires investing some capital in revenue streams and enterprises outside the global financial system.

Investing in a mine 6,000 miles away is different from investing in a mine you can visit and verify with your own eyes.

Investing in an enterprise 6,000 miles away about which you know nothing other than Wall Street trades its shares is different from investing in a business listed on a local exchange that you can visit and research locally.

Investing in a fund of far-flung corporate interests which are "verified" by self-referential Wall Street facades of "trust" that do not verify anything other than a systemic intent to misrepresent risk is different from investing in assets you control or in cooperatives and enterprises in which you have an operational say.

The essential idea of diversification is that spreading capital over a variety of assets will lower the risk of cataclysmic loss should any one investment sour. But if all the investments are equally risky or in assets that trade together, then diversification will not actually lower risk, it will only create an illusion of lower risk.

True diversification requires investing in a spectrum of non-correlated assets (i.e. they don't rise and fall in parallel) with low real risk and high perceived risk. This means the risk of losing capital is actually low, but the high perceived risk means the yield offered to take on the risk is outsized.

A diversified portfolio seeks assets with asymmetrically low real risk, high perceived risk, low entry costs and low opportunity costs.

16 | Building Social and Human Capital

Just as the economic landscape has become a barren monoculture dominated by Colonial Plantation Stores and other centralized cartels, so too has the social capital ecosystem withered as the citizenry have become dependent on the Central State and global corporations.

The postwar era was dominated by an unspoken directive: the more centralized, the better. Corporations gathered mass via endless acquisitions, and the Central State gained control over more and more of the economy and the society. But this dynamic has run its course, and centralization reaps increasingly marginal return. As a result, where dependence on highly centralized concentrations of financial and political power—the government and global corporations—was once considered the path to security, such dependence is now a risky pathway to ruin as monoculture concentrations of power are intrinsically unstable.

Stability and security now arise from decentralized, distributed, open-source, voluntary, transparent, self-organizing networks.

Many people have little or no financial capital. This does not mean they have no capital: if they are unemployed or underemployed, then they have time which can be invested in social and human capital.

As I have noted above, concentrations of political power and wealth are simply two sides of the same coin. Extreme concentrations of wealth and power lead to stagnation and instability both in the economy and the society. Investing time in supporting these extreme concentrations of wealth puts you on the wrong side of history, as these concentrations of power and wealth will follow the Supernova pathway to implosion.

In pre-Savior-State eras, people relied not on welfare (individual or corporate) doled out by a centralized Savior State but on local networks of self-help and mutual benefit. I described these models in *Survival+*, and noted that their key building block is reciprocity: members don't just extract value, they contribute value.

In a society dominated by the Savior State, people have been trained to extract benefits, and to focus their energy and time on gaming the system to maximize their extraction. As a result, the idea that you should contribute value before attempting to extract value has become an alien concept in the U.S.

Reciprocity doesn't exist in a monoculture dominated by the Savior State; two traits characterize such a society: 1) victimhood is rewarded, as being a victim qualifies one to extract "free" benefits from the State, and 2) State coercion via taxation and the restriction of civil liberties. Just as "free enterprise" is a façade masking a de facto system of State-approved crony capitalist cartels, so Savior State oppression is cloaked by regulations and a shadow system of finance and political influence. Just as in "banana republics," dictatorships, oligarchies and theocracies, there are two sets of rules: a hidden set for the Power Elites controlling concentrations of wealth and political power, and a published set for the lower 99%.

The first step to escaping this oppression is to relinquish the victimhood mindset and its goal of extracting value without contributing equivalent value.

As noted above, this atrophied view of self and community leads to a mono-mania with concentrating personal wealth and "looking out for Number One."

In traditional societies, an obsessive concern with "looking out for Number One" was recognized as a narcissistic pathology incapable of empathy, and thus a grave danger to everyone in the community. A single-minded devotion to "Looking out for Number One" would earn the unfortunate sociopath a quick passage to banishment. In a world in which the community offered the only security, banishment was the equivalent of a death sentence.

In essence, our cultural worship of maximizing profit and amassing concentrations of wealth and power renders us a pathological society. Our acceptance of a coercive Savior State which exacts tribute and doles out benefits based on victimhood and corruption is also deeply pathological. Both of these cultural directives reward narcissism, victimhood, fraud and dysfunctional dependence, and both place no value on empathy or reciprocity.

The State and global corporation are both incapable of caring, and thus both are incapable of recognizing empathy and reciprocity, much less valuing those traits.

The foundation of social capital is reciprocity: contributing value first and then reaping the returns from that investment.

Investments in social and human capital carry the same risks as financial investments: you might invest significant time in a project and extract precious little value from the investment. This is why it is important that your choice of social and human investment is based on self-expression: earning another degree because someone else set that goal for you will probably yield a poor return.

Investing time and energy in building social capital is not charity: the goal is to invest in something with a return. The key feature of social capital is that there are many forms of return: experience, contacts, friendship, and so on. Another feature of social capital is that the return might not be the one you anticipated, or it might yield results down the road in some unexpected fashion.

Investing in social and human capital has another feature: it engages you in rewarding activity and networking. Who is the happier person, the one sitting home alone restlessly switching distractions from TV to the Web to videogames and then back, or the one productively engaged with others in their community?

Since health is the one real wealth, we might ask if there is a connection between health and human and social capital. The answer is yes, and that shouldn't surprise us. Research has found that the most important factor distinguishing happy men from their unhappy brethren is long-term friendships: the unhappy men have only superficial acquaintances. Sociologists consider meaningful friendship a form of "social attachment," but that term doesn't do justice to friendship as one of the highest forms of social capital.

Social capital can be understood as a metric of trust. Trust is, after all, an essential component of friendship, community and enterprise alike. Social capital is based on the ecosystem model, in which personal fulfillment, improvements to health and return on investment all share connections and nodes.

If we compare a flourishing, vibrant community with a poverty-stricken one, we find that the difference in wealth is not just a matter of money. The poor community is not just lacking in money; there is a poverty of trust, reciprocity and enterprise, and an abundance of distrust, resentment and debilitating dependence on Savior State handouts, and a resultant atmosphere of defeat and surrender.

This poverty of social capital is directly related to economic poverty and dependence on the Savior State. In terms of an ecosystem, a poor community is a wasteland lacking self-supporting networks of social capital, a landscape devoid of enterprise except the Plantation Store. There are few avenues for investing in human and social capital, and efforts to build networks are hampered by lack of trust and a culture of victimhood.

A lack of financial capital does not necessarily doom a community to stagnation and poverty, but a lack of social and human capital most surely does.

Marketing the value system of maximizing extraction to concentrate personal wealth and power is the first essential step in exploiting a community and making it subservient to outside capital. This value system erodes social capital and takes a prosperous, self-sustaining community of small landholders and shopkeepers and turns it into a wasteland dominated by a few corporate owners of seaside resorts and farms, which then offer low-paying jobs to the disenfranchised locals. As the community is flooded with cheap corporate capital, costs rise, and local residents find they have to take a low-paying job to earn enough cash to live. Global cartels flush with "free money" from central banks strip-mine the sea and buy up all the land, depriving locals of their ownership and non-cash livelihoods.

Understanding this dynamic of exploitation is important, for without that understanding it is difficult to grasp the full value of social capital.

How does one invest in social and human capital? By becoming deeply engaged in projects which are forms of self-expression and by aligning those projects with your longer-term goals.

Engagement and Mastery

Much of what passes for "networking" in today's society is superficial—brief, disconnected gatherings aimed at getting a corporate job. Engagement begins with an abiding interest that is fueled by a willingness to get your hands dirty with the nitty-gritty work of groups and projects.

In a similar fashion, "human capital" is often reduced to costly formal education: "investing in yourself" is equated with getting another degree. If a field of study is a form of self-expression, and mastery is the goal, then a degree may provide a necessary stepping stone. But mastery typically requires experience, and that is where social capital comes into play.

If you want to learn about entrepreneurial finance, then find a local group of investors that offers "angel" investing and peer-to-peer lending. If you are deeply interested in bicycles and would like to find a paying job working with bikes, then join the local biking organization.

Volunteer to complete a specific, small project as a way of demonstrating commitment, competence and trustworthiness.

If you don't have an interest abiding enough to sustain a goal of mastery, then downgrade that interest to a hobby and seek out another form of self-expression. Without the enthusiasm of self-expression, it is difficult to succeed in any field of endeavor. Enthusiasm and an abiding interest in the field are the foundations of mastery, and all three are needed to generate value.

We cannot borrow others' goals or interests as our own, nor can we successfully compete against enthusiasm with a half-hearted commitment to a field chosen for us by others.

Engagement is not a matter of showing up at an occasional meeting; it is caring about the goals and projects of the group or enterprise, and taking on real projects and seeing them through to completion. That's how social capital works; your commitment, competence and trustworthiness will be noted by others, and you will gain experience in leadership, working with others and a variety of specific skills.

Goals and Projects

What can someone with little to no financial capital or income do in terms of investment? Although this may sound trite, it is actually quite profound: take on a project, see it through, and then move on to the next project.

This may seem "obvious" to those with busy, productive lives, but after losing one's assets and/or job, it is natural to be disheartened, and natural to be feel discouraged by the process of reestablishing an income and capital. It is for these people that I offer this simple tool, for sometimes placing one foot in front of the other can feel like an impossible task.

Feeling better about yourself and your prospects starts with making yourself useful in small ways.

Expand your projects to include social capital—contributing to others in your community or to a local organization or enterprise—and human capital—investing in your own skills and experience.

Ideally, your choice of projects, however small, is aimed at longer-term goals such as mastery of a field or bringing a dream of enterprise to fruition. Once again, setting goals may seem painfully "obvious" to some, but having longer-term goals is one of those characteristics which differentiate the wealthy (and I mean wealthy in health, fulfillment and social capital, not money) from the impoverished.

Everyone wants to feel inspired, to contribute, and to be worthy of respect, caring and admiration. Contributing to your community of friends, neighbors and others who share your values and interests is a way of doing so in a way that is within your control.

My own ongoing small projects include picking up the trash which gathers on my block from inconsiderate passersby, and maintaining a multitude of flowers for public view in my property. Flowers are abundant in prosperous, happy communities and completely lacking in poverty-stricken unhappy ones. The connection is not random.

These simple projects add to the community in small but significant ways, and I can pursue them at near-zero expense and without official permission or funding from some government agency.

What projects should you pursue? The only person who can answer that question is you. Seek out what inspires you and generates enthusiasm within you of its own accord. Look to what you do every day, for as Aristotle observed, "We are what we repeatedly do." Put another way: we are what we do every day, and what we do every day in service of a long-term goal is the path to mastery.

17| Relative Value/Performance

Relative value (the concept is also known as relative performance or relative strength) is a simple idea: the most useful way to establish the value of anything is by measuring it against another tangible commodity or the purchasing power of labor.

What's the point of relative value/relative performance? For investors, it's this: when something is relatively undervalued, then it becomes a low-risk opportunity--a buy. When it is relatively overvalued, then it becomes high-risk, i.e. ripe for a sell or hedge. In entrepreneurial terms, relative value helps us shift capital from low productivity enterprise to higher productivity enterprise.

In household terminology, when assets are undervalued, then they are "on sale."

Another way of understanding relative value as an investment tool is to see profitable investing as the process of identifying asymmetric valuations. In symmetric valuations, risk and the potential gain are roughly equal: modest risk exposes the owner to modest gains, and high risk exposes the owner to potentially outsized gains.

 Put another way: the ideal investment has two parts. The first is that "risk has been wrung out" of the asset; in other words, the risk of it declining further is low. The second part is the potential return or gain is high.

An example many of us can relate to is real estate. During non-bubble eras, buying a house exposed a buyer to a small risk of the value declining modestly and an equally small probability of a substantial gain. Early in a bubble era, then the risk of a decline remains low, but the gain is potentially very substantial. At the end of the bubble, just before it bursts, then the risk of a major decline is very high, while the prospect of future gains is extremely low. At that point, risk and return are negatively asymmetric.

Relative value/performance can help us identify assets which have fallen in value to the point that risk of further decline is low. It can also help us identify assets which historically have significant upside potential from their relative lows.

On the most basic level, we are practicing relative performance if we stock up on coffee when global supply and demand has pushed its price down to historically low levels: we know it doesn't get much cheaper than this, and that it typically doesn't stay this cheap for long, so we buy more now while it's cheap. Coffee is "on sale," so we stock up, knowing that coffee prices are volatile and the current price is at the low end of the range. Risk of further price reductions is low--risk has been wrung out of coffee's valuation—but future increases in value are likely significant. Risk and return are positively asymmetric.

If we wanted to act on this as investors, we could purchase coffee futures on the commodity exchange.

In the normal course of daily life, we assess value of tangible goods in our national currency, i.e. the dollar. But measuring value in currencies like the dollar, euro, yen or renminbi is profoundly misleading, as every currency fluctuates in purchasing power. Purchasing power is shorthand for how much of a tangible good can be purchased with a unit of currency.

Put another way, currencies fluctuate in value just like tangible goods and stocks, and so what we assume is a solid foundation—our currency—is in fact just another volatile commodity that rises and falls with supply and demand on the global stage.

Here are some examples to illustrate the misleading nature of valuing anything in currency.

Hours of Labor, Inflation and Purchasing Power

In 1976, the year after I graduated from university, I earned about $14,000, a sum that was close to the national median earnings. Last year (2010) my earned income was about $56,000, or four times my income 35 years ago. Once again this is very close to the median earnings of a male with a bachelor's degree, as measured by the U.S. Census Bureau.

The Bureau of Labor Statistics tracks inflation, and according to their calculations, it takes $4 to buy what $1 purchased in 1976. So my earnings rose in lockstep with inflation.

Since "inflation" has all sorts of connotations, it is more accurate to speak in terms of purchasing power: what our labor can buy in the real world. Since 1976, the dollar has lost so much purchasing power that we must earn four times more dollars just to maintain the purchasing power of our labor.

Since I am earning four times more money now, am I four times wealthier? We all know the answer is no. Since prices also quadrupled, all I did was stay even.

Various studies claim that median income has risen by 44% or more since 1976, adjusted for inflation, which is another way of claiming that I can buy 44% more tangible goods and services than I could in 1976 with the same number of hours of labor. Yet this is patently false. Measured by purchasing power, I can buy less with $56,000 today than I could with $14,000 in 1976. If you study the data, you will reach the same conclusion: 90% of wage earners are poorer in terms of purchasing power than they were in 1976 even though their earnings in dollars have quadrupled.

Rather than indulge in arcane calculations of inflation, hedonic adjustments (when things improve in quality but stay the same in price), household size, and a dizzying array of other factors influencing value priced in dollars, the less misleading approach is to measure things in terms of hours of labor.

For example, tuition and student fees at the University of Hawaii in 1975 totaled $234 a year. My hourly wage was $7 per hour, so it required about 33.4 hours of labor to pay my annual tuition and student fees (not including books or other expenses).

Today, the tuition and fees total about $4,000 per year. I earn about $28 per hour, so it would require 142.8 hours of labor to pay the tuition and fees—over four times more than in 1975.

This example reveals that if we cut through the obfuscations of inflation calculations, university tuition now costs four times more than it did 35 years ago.

Here is another example. The average house cost about $40,000 in 1976, according to U.S. Census Bureau data, so it required 5,714 hours at my 1976 wage rate to buy a house. In December 2008, the average house price was $301,000, or 10,750 hours of labor at my current rate. This shows that in December 2008, the average house cost almost 90% more than it did in 1975 when measured in the purchasing power of hours of labor.

In terms of rent, it took 18 hours of labor to pay for my cramped studio apartment in 1976, and now an equivalent space in the same neighborhood requires at least 23.5 hours of labor, a 30% increase.

These examples show that the purchasing power of labor has dramatically decreased when it comes to education and housing.

One final example: healthcare. Adjusted for age—that is, comparing the cost of health insurance for a 57-year old male in 1976 to the cost today—basic no-frills health insurance now requires at least three times more hours of labor than it did in 1976.

A few things such as electronics require fewer hours of labor now than they did in 1976, and the capability of the devices is astronomically higher in many cases. In 1984, it required 190 of labor to buy my first Apple Macintosh computer; in 2011, a mere 18 hours of labor were enough to purchase a standard Hewlett-Packard desktop computer that has processing and memory capabilities orders of magnitude beyond the first Mac.

But that sort of "hedonic adjustment" is also misleading, as we only buy a television or computer every few years, while we pay for housing and healthcare every month.

The point of this exercise is to illustrate that measuring value in terms of a currency is profoundly misleading. Simply put, we cannot properly assess the value of something if we refer only to its price in dollars; we must price it in hours of labor or another universally traded commodity such as gold or oil.

Hours of Labor, Gold and Oil

To further our understanding of relative value/performance, let's ask these questions:
1) How many hours of labor are required to buy an ounce of gold?
2) How many hours of labor are required to buy a barrel of crude oil?
3) How many barrels of crude oil are required to buy an ounce of gold?

If we chart the answers over time, we can plot a line that fluctuates with the relative value of the two commodities being correlated: in the first question, labor and gold.

If we take the average hourly earnings of private-sector production workers as a baseline—currently about $19.40—then in June 2011 it takes 79 hours of labor to buy an ounce of gold. In 2001, it took about 20 hours of labor to buy an ounce and back at the peak of gold's nominal price in 1981, it required 100 hours of labor to buy an ounce.

As I write this, gold is around $1,500 an ounce and oil is around $100 a barrel, so it takes about five hours of labor to buy a barrel of oil, and about 15 barrels of oil to buy an ounce of gold.

What's the point of these comparisons of relative value? Simply that they help us identify asymmetric valuations, points when a commodity is historically undervalued or overvalued. If our goal is to buy low-risk investments and exit high-risk ones, then we want to buy things that are undervalued and sell things that are overvalued.

Over time, the gold-oil ratio has moved in a volatile fashion from over 25 to under 8. When it above 25—an ounce of gold buys 25 barrels of oil-- then oil is "cheap" relative to gold, and below 8, it is "expensive" relative to gold, as an ounce of gold only buys 8 barrels of oil.

Here is the somewhat confusing part. We can also read this as gold being "cheap" when the ratio is under 8 and "expensive" when it above 25.

This may seem convoluted compared to pricing gold and oil in dollars, but here's why it's useful to do so.

Any practical investment strategy combines an assessment of risk—that is, how much we're being paid to take on risks—and an assessment of relative value: are we overpaying for assets or are they "on sale" compared to historical valuations?

There are innumerable measures of "value," and most revolve around the ratio of the asset's valuation in dollars (or other currency) to its yield (profit, dividend, etc.). The problem with this approach is that profit margins undergo contraction and expansion. At the top of bubble manias, speculators gladly buy assets with very low yields on the premise that fast growth far outweighs yield as a measure of value.

At market troughs, the few souls buying assets with high yields are fighting a widespread perception that the assets in question have a high risk of declining in value, regardless of their yield.

If the premise that volatility will increase and rules will be changed holds true, then the utility of conventional metrics of valuation based on price-to-earnings (PE) may decline.

Relative performance provides a sturdy platform for assessing value, and that is why it has long been a mainstay tool of professional money managers.

Returning to the gold-oil ratio: When gold was around $300 in 1998, and oil fell to $12/barrel, then the ratio briefly hit 27.5: one ounce of gold could buy 27.5 barrels of oil. Priced in gold, oil was undervalued.

At the other extreme, when oil hit $147/barrel in the summer of 2008 and gold was around $925/ounce, then the ratio fell to 6.25: one ounce of gold would buy only 6.25 barrels of oil. Priced in gold, oil was overvalued.

The basic idea of charting this ratio is to assess when oil is "cheap" or "expensive" when priced in gold, and when gold is cheap when priced in oil. When gold is relatively "cheap" compared to oil, the speculator sells oil and buys gold. When oil is relatively "cheap" compared to gold, so the speculator sells gold and buys oil.

Charted in dollars, both oil and gold have risen, but at uneven rates. Buying oil when the ratio was 25 led to outperformance, and selling oil and buying gold when the ratio hit 8 also led to outperformance, when measured in gold, oil or dollars.

Here is a real-world example. In December 2008, as the global financial crisis took a toll on stocks, gold and oil, oil sank to $32/barrel and gold slipped to around $750 an ounce. Which was the lower-risk investment? If we consulted the gold-oil chart, the spike above 25 suggested that oil was even more undervalued than gold and thus the investment in oil was more likely to outperform.

Since then, gold has doubled when priced in dollars, but oil has tripled. With the gold-oil ratio at around 15, neither gold nor oil appears undervalued or overvalued.

Priced in hours of labor, oil bottomed in late 2008 at two hours of labor to buy a barrel of oil and gold troughed at 40 hours of labor to buy an ounce.

This is an example of using two well-known commodities to seek asymmetric values, but there are many other possibilities. The basic idea here is that relative value is a tool. Unlike "one size fits all" advice, a tool must be used to understand how it works. That is the job of everyone who takes control of their own investing.

Even if you don't want to study relative-performance charts, the key concepts presented here will help your assessments of perceived and real risk.

Gold, Stocks and Purchasing Power

Another commonly used measure of relative value is to compare stocks and gold. This is often phrased as: how many "shares" of the Dow Jones Industrial Average (DJIA) will one ounce of gold buy? In the week of January 10, 2000, the DJIA hit a multiyear high of 11,722. Gold was around $300 an ounce, so the Dow/gold ratio was about 39: it required 39 ounces of gold to buy a "share" of the Dow at 11,722.

In the week of January 10, 2011, the Dow hit 11,787, about the same level it had reached 11 years earlier. But since gold was $1,380/ounce, the Dow/gold ratio was 8.5: it required only 8.5 ounces of gold to buy a "share" of the Dow.

Priced in gold, the DJIA lost roughly 80% of its value from 2000 to 2011.

This leads to an important distinction between nominal value and real value. Nominal value is the price in currency (the dollar). In nominal terms, the S&P 500 (SPX) is currently 1,350 and gold is $1,500 an ounce. But if we ask what a "share" of the SPX can buy in oil, gold, loaves of bread or other real goods, then we get a measure of real value.

As noted above, the Bureau of Labor Statistics (BLS) is tasked with calculating inflation. A number of analysts have amassed evidence that the Federal government has understated the true rate of inflation. For simplicity's sake, let's take the BLS statistic as one potentially valid measure of many.

According to the BLS, it takes $1.30 in 2011 to buy what $1 bought in 2000. Thus an asset would have needed to yield 30% over that time just to retain its purchasing power. The broad-based S&P 500 (SPX) hit a high of 1,527 in the week of March 20, 2000, and in May of 2011, it touched 1,370. In nominal terms, the SPX has declined about 160 points, or about 10.4%. Factoring in the 30% decline in purchasing power due to inflation, then the loss is about 40%.

The dividend yield of the SPX is around 2%, which compounded for 11 years from 2000 to 2011 yielded about 24%. This yield offsets the loss, reducing it to about 16%.

Nominally, holding the S&P 500 from 2000 to 2011 registered a loss of capital of 10.4% and a yield of 24%.

In real terms, i.e. adjusted for inflation, then the yield did not keep up with inflation. Holding the SPX led to a decline in purchasing power of 16%. When measured in oil or gold, i.e. how many "shares" of the S&P

500 could be bought with an ounce of gold or a barrel of oil, then the loss is much more severe, roughly 2/3.

If we ask how many loaves of bread a "share" of the SPX could buy in 2000 and in 2011, we find that stocks did not hold their purchasing power when priced in bread, which according to the BLS cost $1 a loaf in 2001 and $1.37 a loaf in 2011.

Priced in eggs, stocks did even worse, as eggs rose by almost 80%.

This exercise shows that nominal measures of stock market returns are misleading, and the only way to properly assess value is with purchasing power: what our labor and capital can buy in the real world.

Relative Value of Labor, Bread, Gold and Housing

As individuals, we can invest our time and our scarce capital (cash) in a variety of things. Investing in ways to increase the value of our labor is one option. This includes a range of possibilities, from gaining a trade certification or university degree to building a sole proprietorship enterprise.

If we look at the relative value of labor over the past 30 years, we find that it is declining except for the top 10% of the populace with professional jobs and/or capital that generates substantial "rentier" (passive) returns. This leads many to conclude that an advanced degree offers a ticket to the top level of income. But the unemployment rate for many classes of PhD degree holders is 50%, and recent surveys have found that 25% of retail clerks have college degrees. The devaluation of labor appears to be so broad-based that the traditional highways to joining the professional class have narrowed and become choked with competitors.

The calculation of relative value can thus be applied to the value of investing in traditional education, the cost of which is rising at three times the rate of inflation. For example, a college degree that costs $120,000 and yields a low-paying retail job is a poor investment. Are there other investments in one's earning capacity which offer a better return on the time and capital invested than a traditional college degree? An analysis based on relative value leads us to assess the costs, risks and return of every major investment.

As the relative costs of food, housing, medical care, education, etc. rise compared to labor, this also implies that it is increasingly difficult to save money, i.e. accumulate capital. This also suggests that the potential return on investments made in real goods and services might outperform purely financial investments.

In other words, $20,000 invested in a micro-business that requires labor (time), skills and capital (savings) that produces real goods and services might end up yielding a much better return than borrowing $120,000 for a traditional college degree that leads to a low-paying job without many prospects of advancement.

This is not to denigrate the non-financial value of a university education, or to suggest that an investment of $120,000 in a university degree is a poor one; it is simply to suggest that assessing the relative value of any investment is a useful exercise.

I will close this discussion of relative value with an anecdote. An old friend of mine once proposed that the way to assess whether housing was overpriced would be to calculate how many loaves of bread it takes to buy a median-priced house.

In 1980, according to the U.S. Census Bureau, the median home price in the U.S. (unadjusted for inflation) was $47,200. Thus it required 89,000 loaves of bread, at 53 cents a loaf, to buy a house. In 2000, bread was $1 a loaf and the median house was $119,600, so it required almost 120,000 loaves of bread to buy a house.

Currently, the median home price is about $166,000 and bread is $1.37 a loaf, so it takes 121,000 loaves to buy a house. Priced in bread, housing is more expensive than it was in 2000, but not by much. As our labor is buying less bread, and also less housing, both are more expensive in terms of labor.

What would it take for this ratio to adjust so that it took 40,000 loaves of bread to buy a median-priced house? Either bread (wheat) could triple or housing could decline by two-thirds, or bread could rise and nousing could fall.

Priced in gold, i.e. how many ounces of gold are required to buy a house, it took about 370 ounces of gold in 2000 to buy a median-priced home. In 2010, it required only 130 ounces of gold to buy a median-valued house. Priced in dollars, the median home cost more in 2010 than it did in 2000, but gold rose more than housing. Put another way, gold outperformed housing and bread as an investment.

What is cheap and what is dear? Nominal valuations don't offer much help. There are no hard and fast answers, but comparing various asset classes, yields and liquidity (how easily can we sell the service or asset) can help us discern what appears to be undervalued ("on sale") in historical terms and what appears to be overvalued.

The investor mentioned earlier who day-trades silver mining companies uses this same idea: he buys the company which has underperformed its peers and then sells it for a profit when it outperforms on a relative basis. The tool of assessing relative value works on all time lines, short, medium and long-term, and on a broad spectrum of investments.

Selling what is currently overpriced and high-risk and investing in what is currently underpriced and low-risk is a time-tested formula for outperformance.

18 |　Assessing the Value of Local Assets

What happens if global stock markets lose 50% or more of their value in a few months?

If you don't have any money in those markets, then nothing happens: you insulated yourself from those risks by not having any capital invested in global stock markets.

What happens if the Federal government rations oil and gasoline due to scarcity?

If you don't need much gasoline to operate your enterprise or get to work/school/shopping, then the impact of rationing would be minimal because you insulated yourself from the global oil market by living close by work, school, shopping, etc.

What happens if the Federal government restricts the medical care covered by Medicare?

If you did all you could to stay healthy and accumulated some capital and independent sources of income, then you are well-prepared to pay for your own medical care.

What if the government cuts all pay and benefits in half? Could you live on 50% of your government check?

What if the government revalues the dollar and all money is suddenly worth 10% of its previous value?

What if the government once again outlaws/expropriates all privately held gold and silver?

You see the point: dependence on concentrations of power--the Central State, centralized stock and energy markets—and on any one asset class creates extreme vulnerability. The more dependent we are on factors outside our control, the more vulnerable we are to systemic instability. The less we rely on distant suppliers and a devolving Central State, and the more essentials we control, the lower our risk and the greater our resilience.

In our ecosystem model, depending on the Central State and heavy consumption of oil is like being dependent on a single distant food source: if that food source vanishes from the system, we vanish, too. Resilience is like being an omnivore—the broader the spectrum of foods we eat, the lower of risk of want and malnutrition. As an obvious corollary, the more foods we raise and have access to in our local ecosystem, the lower the risks of starvation.

This same principle applies to capital and income: the more types of capital we control and invest synergistically, the less vulnerable we are to systemic instability. The more varied our income streams, the greater our resilience to systemic disruption. Dependence is like an intrinsically precarious monoculture, independence and self-reliance are traits of adaptable, resilient ecosystems.

In a similar way, a household that needs 99% of its income just to maintain its status quo is terribly vulnerable to any disruption in income or increase in expenses. In contrast, the household that can get by on 50% of household income can survive drastic cuts in income or increases in expenses and still prosper. The same can be said of enterprises; those with high cost structures are pushed into insolvency by any disruption.

Compare a household that needs a barrel of gasoline (42 gallons) a week, transported from the Mideast or other distant places, just to maintain the bare essentials of transport to work, school, grocery shopping, etc., with one where the household residents could reach these destinations on bicycles, skis, public transport or on foot, or could pool resources with neighbors to slash their oil consumption by 50% or even 75% in short order.

At today's low prices for fossil fuels, the idea of owning energy sources such as solar panels or windmills is generally mocked as an inefficient waste of money. This may well be true, until supposedly abundant energy from distant lands is suddenly scarce. What is the value of owning resources? The real value is only realized when supply chains of "cheap, abundant energy" are disrupted.

Charging an electric bicycle or golf cart from locally produced sources of electricity makes no sense as long as cheap energy from abroad is abundant; but if that ever changes, then what was mocked as foolish will suddenly look prudent. Since North America has abundant natural gas, then those who align their consumption with what is locally abundant—for example, by owning a vehicle that burns natural gas instead of gasoline—will be far less vulnerable to disruption than those who depend on resources shipped from unstable regimes overseas.

The same is true of food: locally grown food can be dismissed as financially nonsensical as long as cheap oil enables cheap food to be flown or trucked in from afar. But we don't control these distant resources, and so the resilience of these long supply chains is illusory.

As the ancient Chinese proverb noted, "When you're thirsty, it's too late to dig a well." The entire point of this book is to encourage diversification of capital and income as the Status Quo destabilizes, rather than wait for crisis and then wonder what to do.

All of this speaks to three principles, all of which seek to lower risk and increase resiliency in an era of systemic instability: the value of local control, the value of broad-based "ecosystems" of capital and income, and the reduction of risk via the reduction of dependency on long supply chains and centralized sources of income.

As global instability becomes the norm, the value of local assets will rise. Not all local, decentralized assets are equal in value and risk, however, so being able to assess those is a necessary investment tool.

In other words, local assets are not intrinsically lower in risk than global assets; many investors lose all their capital by investing in a local restaurant or other high-risk venture. Indeed, it's remarkably easy to lose an investment in local ventures. The key point is that assets you control directly or through direct ownership are qualitatively different from passive ownership of global markets. If you control your capital and assets, then you can take steps to lower risk and increase return. The risks are more transparent than the purposefully obscured risk of global markets, and thus easier to assess and manage.

As we assess the risk and value of any asset, local or global, we should always keep in mind that cash is also an asset, and that sometimes cash is the lowest-risk trade available. We should also keep in mind the primary monetary agenda of the Status Quo mentioned earlier: if the central banks/States succeed in creating inflation, how can we maintain our purchasing power? And if they fail to engineer stable inflation, then how do we survive the black holes of hyperinflation or systemic credit default?

They key difference between a local asset and a global market asset is the global assets are traded in fiat currency such as the dollar. If all paper currencies are eventually devalued by high inflation, revaluation or hyperinflation, then the value of those global-market assets will be contingent on all sorts of issues outside of our control.

Compare that uncertainty and potential exposure to catastrophic loss to owning a pear orchard, for example. It really doesn't matter if the currency used to buy the harvest is the dollar, the euro or the quatloo, or if the buyer trades gold or wheat or hours of labor for pears: the pears will retain the same value regardless, a value established by supply and demand. If pears are abundant and demand is low, the price fetched will be relatively low; if supply is low and demand is strong, then the price will be relatively high. The crop may be rendered near-worthless by supply and demand, but it won't be rendered worthless by central bank manipulations or global financial instability.

If it takes $1,000 to buy a loaf of bread or ten cents to buy the same loaf, the pear harvest will retain the same relative value to a loaf of bread. If the dollar is reduced to worthlessness, the pear harvest will still be worth the same when measured by hours of labor or gold.

As long as the Central State doesn't expropriate the orchard and the owner has no debt that can be called, then the orchard will pass through the black holes of devaluation, State default or hyperinflation intact. The day after the crisis passes, the trees will still be producing pears, just as they did before the crisis. How many zeros are printed on the paper exchanged for the harvest changes nothing: the purchasing power of the harvest, and thus the value of the orchard, remains intact.

This illustrates the key differences between financial assets entrusted to global markets and tangible, debt-free assets that produce income streams in the local real economy.

The Cycle of Dependency on Central Authority and the Atrophy of Self-Reliance

In his book *Collapse of Complex Societies*, anthropologist Joseph Tainter identified two causes of economic collapse: investments in social complexity yield diminishing returns, and energy subsidies, i.e. cheap, abundant energy, decline. In my terminology, the dynamic he describes is one in which the cost structure of a society continues rising due to "the ratchet effect" but the gains from the added expenses are increasingly marginal.

At some point the additional costs, usually justified as the "solution" to the marginal returns problem, become counterproductive and actually drain the system of resilience as dissent and adaptability ("variation is information") are suppressed. This feeds systemic instability: on the surface, all seems stable, but beneath the surface, the potential for a stick/slip destabilization grows unnoticed.

Cheap, abundant energy offers a surplus of value that can be invested in social complexity and consumption. Once the cost and availability of energy declines, then that surplus shrinks and can no longer be used to support the high cost structure.

The U.S. and other economies have clearly been driven to the cliff edge of instability by both dynamics: the cheap, abundant energy which enabled fast growth of consumption and high cost social complexity is vanishing, and the cost structure of the economy has ballooned far beyond sustainability.

To recount two previously mentioned examples: the "best of the best" fighter aircraft that cost $56 million per plane only a few years ago is being replaced by a new aircraft that costs $300 million each. Medicare/Medicaid and other healthcare costs are growing at two to three times faster than the underlying economy, and now consume twice as much per capita as any other developed nation. The "solution" offered by the Status Quo is a horrendously costly layer of additional complexity.

Put another way, the institutions that were intended to solve society's big problems slip into self-preservation, and thus end up adding to costs and problems alike.

Jared Diamond's book *Collapse: How Societies Choose to Fail or Succeed* argues persuasively that environmental mismanagement plays a key role in social instability and collapse. Some of the key factors include the relative fragility of the ecosystem, the human population's demands on the carrying capacity of the environment, and the ability of social institutions to effectively problem-solve ecological overshoot.

In my analysis, there is a third dynamic that causes societies to cycle through growth, stasis and decline: an unremarked cycle of rising dependency on the Central State for direction, distraction and the essentials of life.

One example of this is the Roman Empire, which experienced an atrophying of enterprise and innovation as the Empire increased taxation on its remaining productive enterprises to fund the Empire's high cost structure. To quell dissent, the Empire pursued a dual strategy of increased political oppression and placating the increasingly dependent lower classes with "bread and circuses," literally distributing free bread and free entertainment to roughly 40% of the population of Rome. Both of these strategies required additional expenditures of treasure, even as they suppressed the dissent and adaptation (i.e. the information in variation) that might have led to a successful "ratchet down" transition to a much less costly and sustainable decentralized structure.

These tactics also create a third pernicious dynamic: as dependence on the Central State rises, self-confidence and self-reliance both decline, sapping the populace of the confidence and drive needed to meet the challenges of diminishing returns and higher energy costs.

We can visualize rising dependence on the Savior State and

declining self-reliance on a see-saw: as dependence rises, self-confidence and self-reliance must fall.

What ensues is a classic destructive dynamic of co-dependence in which the supplicants demand ever more "bread and circuses" even as their resentment over their dependent status rises unabated. The Central State eventually taxes the productive citizenry into penury, as the poor are now completely dependent on the Savior State and the wealthy escape taxation via bribes and favoritism.

It seems clear to me that the U.S. is in the final stages of just such a dependency cycle that will end in the implosion of the Central Savior State as its obligations far exceed the economy's ability to generate surpluses on that gigantic scale. As noted earlier, the Central State can always print money, but this artifice doesn't "fool Mother Nature" for long; it doesn't matter how many zeros are printed on the paper, the product will still cost the same in terms of energy and hours of labor.

The end result of money-printing that is unsupported by actual surplus generated by the economy is the government sends out checks for $1,000 every month in accordance with its obligations but that sum only buys a single loaf of bread. You cannot fool Mother Nature by printing bits of paper and claiming they are a future claim on real goods and services unless the extra money is based on additional surplus being added to the system.

This dynamic leads to an environment in which citizens expect jobs, healthcare, housing, education, etc. from a Central State whose cost has already exceeded the carrying capacity of the economy. As cheap, abundant energy disappears, then the Central State loses a key subsidy of its bloated complexity. As the State's fiefdoms devote their remaining energy to self-preservation at the expense of taxpayers or other fiefdoms, the problem-solving potential of these institutions drops below zero: not only can they not solve any pressing problems, their "ratchet effect" efforts at self-preservation actively create new layers of problems and costs which push the State closer to insolvency.

Rather than wait for the Savior State to renege on its impossible promises, this book suggests pushing the see-saw in the other direction: boost self-reliance and self-confidence and lower dependence on a Savior State doomed by unfavorable demographics, high cost structure, failed institutions and rising energy costs.

Seeking diverse, non-complex income streams and a diversity of local supply options for essentials are key strategies for raising self-reliance. Lowering the household's cost structure and weaning the household from total dependence on the Savior State and long supply chains for energy is the other side of the see-saw.

Functional, Intrinsic and Relative Value

To properly value local assets, we need to understand the concept of functional utility. I use this term not as a strict econometric definition but to describe a very basic notion: things provide utility or usefulness in varying degrees, and depending on supply and demand, the ease of trade and the risks involved, they have tradable value and generate an income stream.

Put another way: these assets produce something of value which can be sold or traded. Desirable shelter generates rent, farmland produces a crop, a wind turbine generates electricity, a café provides prepared food and a dining experience, etc. Human capital also produces value; a barber, dentist, auto mechanic, accountant, etc. all perform services that have tradable value in the market. Social capital can also generate value: one's circle of friends and associates might fund your cafe, and be your initial base of customers.

Direct control of these assets is qualitatively different from owning assets in the global financial system, as the risk we are being paid to take on in global stock and bond markets is intrinsically unknowable, despite official promises of safety, security and trustworthiness. The distant enterprise we have invested in may or may not have functional value, but the electronic connection between that distant value and the value of our investment can be broken by instability, fraud or Central

State intervention.

A second concept is intrinsic value, which is based on the idea that humans consume food, energy and water (what I term the FEW essentials), and they need shelter, security, community and other aspects of civilization that stretch back to the hunter-gatherer and agricultural societies of the distant past. The market value of each thing is in constant flux, as the market price is influenced by supply and demand, the cost of money, etc. Thus even things with intrinsic value can temporarily fall to near-zero. Nonetheless, as a general rule, things which are necessary for life will tend to retain their value more reliably than things which are discretionary.

A third concept is relative value (also known as relative strength, relative performance), which we covered in a previous chapter. Over time, the value of one good fluctuates in relation to the value of other goods. This dynamic is independent of fluctuations in currency such as dollars or euros.

The advantageous trade is to sell the good or service which is relatively overvalued (has greater purchasing power than other goods) and buy those goods which are relatively inexpensive. This is the basis of entrepreneurship: shifting human and financial capital out of lower productivity and into higher productivity. The basic idea here is that assets with functional-utility (income-producing) value are generally more productive and valuable than assets with no utility value or income stream.

The example of a house offers insight into these aspects of valuation.

A house may have intrinsic value as shelter but if it is located in a place with no demand for shelter, then its functional value may be zero. This is visible in rural areas that have been depopulated—abandoned farm houses—and also in depopulated inner cities, where houses have lost functional value despite their intrinsic value as shelter.

Farmland has intrinsic value, but if the land depends on marginal rainfall to be productive, its functional value is considerably lower than land with water rights for irrigation.

Commercial space in a small town has intrinsic value—it once housed a business, and could do so again—but if the town has lost population and its reason to exist, the building has no functional value.

It's easy to mistake intrinsic value for functional value. The difference is the asset with utility value generates an income stream.

Gold as a Special Local Asset and Risk

Physical gold, silver and other precious metals in private hands are local assets, and so I will address the unique characteristics of physical precious metals in this section. (To keep from writing "gold, silver and other precious metals" constantly, I will use the single word "gold" as a proxy for all precious metals. There are of course many differences between the various precious metals, and I use "gold" because it is commonly understood and recognized as a store of value and potentially a means of exchange in one form or another.)

As I will explain further in the section on hedging, gold has a unique value as a hedge against the potentially catastrophic risks in the global financial system. Gold is both money (a means of exchange) and a store of value that fluctuates in relation to energy, food, labor, etc. It does not have a counterparty, that is, some institution which must make good on a claim of value--for example, the U.S. government, which guarantees the Federal Reserve Notes in our wallets will retain their value to buy goods and services.

But gold does not generate an income stream, and thus its value is different from those assets which generate income.

A bit of history helps illustrate the difference. As historian Fernand Braudel described in his three-volume history *Civilization and Capitalism, 15th – 18th Centuries*, the West traded gold and silver to the East (India and China) for silks and other goods. The Western traders then resold the goods for immense profits, which were reinvested in other trades and assets, including credit instruments which earned interest.

In contrast, while the gold and silver sat idly in the vaults of the Eastern potentates as "wealth," those nations' economies stagnated and were soon eclipsed by the mercantilist Capitalist West.

In the very broad view, the East's view of gold and silver as the primary form of wealth doomed it to underperformance compared to the capitalist West, which invested its wealth in expanding trade, technologies and assets which produced income. While the gold and silver sat unproductively in the palaces of the rajas, the capital of the West built factories, leveraged technology, exploited opportunities and earned interest in a well-developed system of tradable joint stock shares and credit instruments—all before the discovery of oil.

There is a place for stores of concentrated wealth, but these cannot replace income-producing assets.

Some people are confident that gold is the only asset that will hold its value in troubled times, but this presumes the owner has some source of income to live on or sufficient gold to sell a percentage off monthly to pay for living expenses. This also presumes that gold will remain legal to own, a right that was revoked by Executive order in 1933 with the stroke of a pen (each person was permitted to own five ounces).

Nobody knows what will happen in the future, and so the best strategy is also unknown; but history suggests that owning a diverse spectrum of assets that includes income-producing enterprises that are within our own control offers the significant advantages of resilience and diversification.

Gold presents a uniquely double-bind risk: if the central banks pursue the strategy of inflating their way out of insolvency, then they may well spark a hyperinflationary spiral that discredits all paper currencies and leaves gold as the only recognized "real money." To say such an outcome is unlikely is one thing, but to claim it is "impossible" is to overlook history.

Current discussions of "sound money" include proposals which would make gold in private circulation the recognized money; in this scenario, the Federal government would sell its Fort Knox gold to the public to facilitate freely circulating gold. Once again, many list this as "impossible," but the next 20 years will be full of "impossible" developments and surprises, and no gold-related idea should be dismissed simply because it differs from the Status Quo conception of money and value.

Other proposals envision a new global currency based on gold and a basket of 30 commodities, along the lines of the global "bancor" currency described by 20th century economist John Maynard Keynes. Once again, any alternatives to the Status Quo of paper dollars as the world's reserve currency are generally dismissed as "unworkable" and "impossible" by conventional economists. Yet as Keynes recognized, the Status Quo's stupendous trade and currency imbalances are ultimately unsustainable, and so what is truly impossible is the Status Quo continuing its current trajectory without an eventual implosion.

Calls for a return to a gold-backed currency in the U.S. are also dismissed as unworkable, i.e. "impossible." Such a "new gold-backed dollar" could plausibly be used as a justification for confiscating privately held gold—i.e., a repeat of the 1933 confiscation.

Here is gold's risk conundrum: it is risky not to own some gold as a hedge against the collapse of the financial Status Quo, yet owning it presents the risk of confiscation by an increasingly desperate Central State.

The irony of gold's proven success in holding value is that this very success as a concentrated store of purchasing power makes it an attractive target for confiscation by the Central State, a "solution" the Federal government turned to in 1933 after a mere four years of Depression. Gold's key characteristic—that it is a physically compact concentration of wealth—means that it would be relatively easy and highly rewarding for the State to confiscate both physical gold and electronically held gold in ETFs or offshore proxies.

Many proponents of holding physical gold are confident that their gold will enable them (and the few other owners of physical-gold wealth left standing after a financial meltdown) to buy up tangible assets at bargain prices.

What is the basis of their confidence that the unique value of gold will escape the notice of the State? If privately owned gold beyond a few ounces is outlawed, then how do you use it to buy tangible assets without exposing it to confiscation? If you can't use it as a means of exchange for productive assets, then what value will it have secreted in a private vault? As for hiding it from the State: a "reward" offered by the State for turning over information on privately held gold might well unearth many private-gold stashes that were considered "secret" by their owners.

Some proponents are confident that such a confiscation would quickly be rescinded due to its dire financial consequences and political unpopularity. Perhaps, but if history is any guide, the vast majority of citizens won't own enough gold to be disaffected, and the top 1/10th of 1% super-wealthy families will have diversified their holdings amongst other nations. (It has been suggested that large quantities of privately held gold were transferred to Switzerland between the announcement of Executive Order 6102 on April 6, 1933 and May 1, 1933, the date citizens were required to relinquish their gold.)

All we can say with certainty is that the 1933 confiscation was not rescinded until 1974 and that it permitted private ownership of collectible coinage and five ounces of gold. Would a future confiscation permit limited ownership? Would gold held in overseas vaults via online/digital accounts be exempt? Would the shares of gold exchange-traded fund proxies such as GLD be exempted? Just as no one knows the probability of a future limitation of private ownership of gold, no one knows what exemptions and limits might be imposed.

As for the possibly dire financial consequences of confiscating "hoarded" gold: it is just as likely that such a seizure would strengthen the Status Quo, or at least buy it some time. Given that roughly 40% of all citizens draw benefits from the Central State, there might actually be widespread support for any move that keeps the Central State from reneging on its promises.

From the point of view of an endangered Central State, the question boils down to: what can we do to preserve the Status Quo with the least cost and risk? Any concentration of wealth makes an attractive target, just as wage earners make the ideal taxpayers because the government can collect a greater share of their income with a simple electronic command, i.e. increase payroll taxes collected by employers.

If we follow various thought experiments, we find that the lower the political power of the owners and the more concentrated the wealth, the higher the rewards to State confiscation.

To take an extreme example, the Central State could seize all privately owned homes. This would alienate 75 million of the nation's 117 million households, and the financial return on that seizure would be modest: what exactly would the State gain by confiscating all private homes? The risk, meanwhile, would be overthrow of the Status Quo: high risk, low return, the classic poor investment.

Even the "slow seizure" of property via crushing property taxes is sufficient to spark political rebellion, as illustrated by California's 1978 Proposition 13 rebellion against ever-higher property taxes.

For an opposing example, consider the nation's handful of rare earth mines. If these strategic metals were at risk of falling into the ownership of foreign powers via corporate proxies, then the Central State might well expropriate the mines in the service of national security. The mines' concentration of wealth would make such a seizure relatively easy, and the owners' political power would be unable to offset the benefits of seizure: these factors combine low risk with high return, the classic wise investment.

It may be that some future gold-backed currency or gold privately held in nations such as Switzerland might escape confiscation, but then the owner would have to secure safe passage to Switzerland to retrieve it and/or transfer it into a form of wealth that remains legal in the U.S. and elsewhere. As for moving to Switzerland to enjoy gold held there: residency rights in traditional gold havens may be more tightly controlled than capital flows.

Should any developed nation with rule of law establish a gold-backed currency and/or the use of gold as currency, and an open-arms immigration policy for those with capital, that nation might soon attract individuals from high-inflation economies seeking to secure the benefits of stable money.

For that is the cruel irony of the Status Quo's policy of engineering inflation: it robs those with the least income and fewest resources by stealing a portion of every paycheck and every saving account.

The ultimate point of this section is to illustrate yet again that there is no risk-free hedge or asset. The future is unknown, and common-sense tells us that highly concentrated portable wealth is an intrinsically attractive confiscation target for an increasingly desperate Central State. This is same principle behind the expectation that the Central State might force privately held retirement funds to buy low-yield government bonds—a slight-of-hand confiscation.

It is also possible that the current (as of mid-2011) expectations of high inflation or hyperinflation are misplaced, and the U.S. dollar will actually increase its purchasing power in the coming years. If this occurs, then gold would become a less valuable hedge. The fact that so few believe this is even remotely possible should alert us to the possibility that current trends will eventually reverse, if for no other reason than the market rarely rewards the majority in a heavily lopsided trade.

As noted in Chapter Three, the entire concept of retaining concentrations of wealth through the coming crises is fraught with difficulties. Decentralized assets of commonly held, diffused value such as houses, small tracts of productive land, local enterprises, etc., are more likely to pass through a full-blown financial meltdown, as their value is based on their income streams and their functional value of supplying basic needs such as food, shelter, energy, etc.

State seizure of decentralized, commonly held assets is so much more costly and risky than confiscation of electronically held and physical gold, and the yield from such a seizure is both politically explosive and financially marginal. What assets are most likely to emerge through a financial/social event horizon? No one can seize experience and social capital, and the seizure value of common assets such as land, local enterprises and houses is intrinsically low to the Central State.

Put another way: a business service or an almond tree yields a harvest regardless of what is used as a means of exchange each season, and its harvest can be traded as a store of value regardless of what else is coveted as a store of wealth.

In other words, the more successful an asset is at retaining purchasing power and the more concentrated it is as a store of wealth, the more likely it is to be confiscated, or subjected to "slow seizure" via taxation, by an insolvent but still powerful Central State. Gold being scarce and concentrated—the financial equivalent of dynamite--makes it the ideal asset to confiscate, hence the rationality of Executive Order 6102 of April 1933, which outlawed "the hoarding of gold coin, gold bullion, and gold certificates within the United States." The order criminalized the possession of monetary gold by any individual, partnership, association or corporation, under penalty of $10,000 fine or ten years imprisonment or both, back when $10,000 could buy several homes.

Is such confiscation now "impossible"? Perhaps we can add it to the long list of other events which were considered "impossible" not long ago that have already come to pass.

Valuing Income Streams

Assessing the value of income streams could easily fill a volume, and so this discussion will only hit the key points. It's important to note that income is simply the surplus left after subtracting expenses from sales. Sales can be paid in cash, gold, silver, tradable goods, hours of labor or services rendered. The medium of exchange is not important, it is the surplus left after paying all expenses that matters.

As always, our goal is fourfold:

-- Move capital out of low-productivity activities and assets and into higher productivity activities and assets

-- Acquire assets when they are undervalued, i.e. "on sale" when measured by relative value

-- Acquire assets and enterprises which produce goods and services with permanent demand, i.e. the basic human necessities in the "hierarchy of needs."

-- Acquire assets and enterprises which produce an income stream

Some income streams are cheaper to maintain and more reliable/resilient than others, and so their value is correspondingly higher. The key valuation factors include:

1) Low maintenance costs, including debt, taxes, and operational expenses. This is common-sense: the higher the minimum expenses, the higher the break-even point and the greater the risk of operational losses. The ideal asset or enterprise has zero debt and low expenses other than time and social capital and generates substantial, reliable income streams. The riskiest asset generates meager or sporadic income and has high debt, energy and maintenance costs.

2) Debt that can be called or the terms modified unilaterally by the lender. Financial leverage works like magic when assets are rising, but if assets fall in value then debt can quickly drag the owner into insolvency. Remember the previously stated adage: it's hard for bad things to happen when you have no debt. The same can be said of expenses in general, especially those over which you have no control.

3) The asset offers non-financial leverage. A movie theater offers an apt analogy. The costs of operating the theater is about the same regardless of how many patrons buy tickets; if only one person shows up for a showing, the theater must still be heated/cooled, the staff present, the popcorn machine operating, etc. Low-cost marketing via email or social media offers leverage: above the break-even point, every additional ticket sold via low-cost social media marketing is profit.

The theater has a limited number of seats, of course, so the total revenue from each showing is limited. If the market for a product or service can be expanded via the Web, then the Web can leverage sales far beyond was possible on a local market, especially if the product or service is digital and shipping is nearly cost-free.

A windmill that powers a water pump might supply a house with domestic water; if it also enabled the planting of a small orchard, then that investment in the windmill would be leveraged from mere consumption into an income stream. Energy and time are forms of capital that can be leveraged, just like financial capital.

4) Enterprises that serve the "hierarchy of needs" will always be in demand, though competition and oversupply could limit revenues and profits.

5) Enterprises that have wide "moats" of startup costs or experience which limit competition will have the advantage of a favorable supply-demand, if their product or service serves the "hierarchy of needs."

6) Low opportunity cost. If an enterprise requires every last dollar to buy and every last hour to operate, it has a very high opportunity cost because every other investment and activity must be sacrificed to pursue this one costly venture. It may be "on sale" by some measures, and perhaps it has an extraordinarily attractive risk-return. But in general, enterprises with low opportunity costs are less risky and less psychologically draining.

7) The process of production or adding value is straightforward and uncomplicated. The more complex the production or value-added process, the more risks are present of disruption: key staff leaves, essential parts break and replacements cannot be found, distant suppliers stop stocking key ingredients, and so on. Complex processes have higher costs and risks. For small enterprises, simple is better; the simpler the process of adding value, the lower the risk and expenses. Complexity acts as a tax and a governor that limits sales and surplus.

8) The supply/sales ecosystem is complex and features many options for obtaining essential inputs and selling the enterprise's products. Reliance on one supplier or long supply chain creates all the risks of a monoculture, including skyrocketing costs and unavailability.

The ideal enterprise has multiple sources of essential ingredients/feedstock, multiple sales channels to sell into, few competitors, low startup costs and low operating/maintenance costs.

9) The enterprise has limited exposure to confiscatory property taxes and "junk fees" by local government. All enterprise is at risk of "slow seizure" by local governments ravenously seeking more tax revenue, but some states limit the annual rise of property taxes, for example, and some counties and cities have histories of maintaining low business fees.

10) The durability of the assets and the enterprise. To use a work-vehicle analogy: the most durable and resilient work vehicle (taxi, truck, etc.) would be a basic ICE (internal combustion) engine fueled by natural gas, the most abundant transport-ready fossil fuel in North America, or an electric vehicle with readily available, hot-swappable batteries. (Recall the fundamental simplicity and efficiency of electric drive and the potential for locally generated electricity.) The least durable vehicle would be a finicky hybrid that the owner cannot maintain himself, that requires high-tech diagnostics tools and complex, costly parts from a long supply chain.

The most durable building is one that's efficient to heat and cool and is constructed of widely available natural materials. The least durable building is a cheaply assembled McMansion that is costly to heat and cool due to its poor design and is constructed of defective drywall and flimsy extruded plastic parts.

Durability yields low maintenance and zero replacement costs, low dependency on long vulnerable supply chains and a wealth of repair options, including do-it-yourself.

An enduring enterprise is built on honesty, reliability and timely delivery of what was promised, low input costs, multiple short supply chains and a product or service of enduring "basic needs" value. Durable assets and enterprises are worth more because that durability translates into lower costs and higher returns.

11) The scalability and flexibility of an enterprise. The ideal enterprise scales up easily to meet increased demand, and ratchets

down equally easily when demand drops without losing its resiliency or quality of service or production.

12) Openness to new models of local credit, trade and cooperation, and openness to global and local innovations. Openness to innovation and the ability to "fail fast, fail small, fail often" is a key feature of adaptable, resilient enterprises.

Other Considerations in Valuing Local Assets

1) At the risk of repetition: financial and energy leverage greatly increases risk. Long supply chains are one form of energy leverage; another is a lifestyle or enterprise with high minimum energy consumption. A lifestyle or enterprise that requires huge quantities of oil just to maintain the Status Quo is like a homeowner with a $2,500 per month adjustable-rate mortgage who makes $3,000 a month: if the rate moves higher, the homeowner is soon bankrupted, regardless of his prudence or frugality in other expenses.

2) The local government is the sea in which enterprises swim—unless social order breaks down completely and there is no local authority. Thus the quality of the local government—city, county and state--is a critical consideration in valuing assets or enterprises.

Many local governments are essentially kleptocracies, parasitical systems that skim substantial percentages of local incomes but provide few services, and those they do provide are low-quality: sporadic, poorly maintained, lacking in accountability or response to the paying public, prone to continuous price increases, junk fees and arbitrary enforcement of complex rules designed to punish any who challenge the oppressive Status Quo. These local kleptocracies enrich a fiefdom or local Elite whose primary goal is self-preservation, whatever the cost to the community.

Enterprises are nothing more than tax donkeys to these local kleptocracies, and the only strategy with any hope of success is to move out of the jurisdiction of these parasitical governments. Once their income base moves away, then they will collapse under their own weight. As legitimate enterprises move away, those that are left will be further taxed and oppressed. Thus it is critical to identify the nature of the local government, as any enterprise burdened with a kleptocracy will be at risk of regulatory and junk-fee strangulation.

Complexity is itself a tax, and so the more overlapping jurisdictions there are skimming fees and adding regulatory burdens, the greater the costs to all enterprises. The more complex the layers of service the local government attempts to provide, the greater the total costs of that government. The ideal local government offers only the most basic services, but does so efficiently and competently.

Not all local governments are corrupt, unresponsive and parasitical. The ideal local government is responsive to those who own and operate small enterprises, and is run by professional managers who understand that regulation of life and safety issues is necessary, but akin to vitamins: a minimum amount does great good, but an excess is harmful. The ideal local government's elected officials understand that government is an enterprise, too, and it exists to serve its clientele, the taxpayers who pay the wages of the government employees. In the ideal local government, all employees are trained to be courteous and responsive, and can readily be fired if courtesy poses an unbearable burden to their conduct. The ideal local government is one where its flexibility and adaptability are not constrained by union contracts forged in a bygone era of debt-based "prosperity," ever-rising tax revenues, and rigid, self-serving work rules.

A low-cost, prudent, honest and accountable local government is a major asset to any enterprise or household. Such a government requires the input and oversight of the productive, honest citizenry, and thus engagement in local government is a requirement of every owner or entrepreneur who understands the value of good governance. If everyone hopes to "free-ride" on local government, that is, avoid taxes and sensible fees and refuses to invest any social capital in issues of governance, then the government will degrade into serving a local Elite or fiefdom, and the capital of all owners and entrepreneurs will be greatly devalued.

3) Any enterprise which depends on a single source or single market is effectually a monoculture, the riskiest, most vulnerable situation. This can be visualized as an inverted pyramid, balancing on its tip: any disruption will cause it to topple over. Enterprises which depend almost solely on government contracts, a single corporate buyer or a single source of key inputs are exquisitely vulnerable to the slightest perturbations: cancelled contracts, government-issued IOUs, contract disputes, supply chain delays or bankruptcy of the sole source or customer.

Enterprises which have an entire ecosystem of multiple suppliers and customers are far more resilient than monocultures.

4) Another aspect of monoculture is isolation: an enterprise which stands alone in its community and whose customers and suppliers are distant will have little local support or "safety nets" is supply chains and distant sales dry up. Connections made over the Web can compensate for this lack of a local network, as can social capital investments in the community.

5) Any machine is only as reliable as its weakest part, and any enterprise is only as resilient as its most vulnerable inputs. Any enterprise which must shut down if one key component or specialized skill is unavailable is a vulnerable and thus risky enterprise. Stockpiles and redundancy can compensate for this dependence on one critical feedstock or component, and in-house training can spread the specialized skill beyond a single worker.

6) The ideal small enterprise leverages a meaningful amount of human and social capital into an income stream with a small investment of scarce financial capital. At the other end of the spectrum, a semiconductor manufacturing plant requires staggering amounts of human capital (expertise) and $2 billion (in 2011 dollars).

Since financial capital is a form of stored energy, the same principle applies to energy: the ideal small enterprise leverages a meaningful amount of human and social capital into an income stream with a small investment of energy.

7) Environments that foster synergy between small startups, local sources of funding, entrepreneurs, producers, established enterprises that are growing, community groups and social enterprises such as cafes, have a hard-to-quantify but very real value, to enterprises which contribute to and gain from those synergies. Synergy is simply another way of saying leverage: a network rich in motivated, smart, experienced people who can draw upon human, social and financial capital provides immense leverage to a new enterprise. Compare an environment bubbling with ideas, enthusiasm, capital and new networks with a listless environment in which the entrepreneur is alone: nobody is interested in new enterprise, there are no other entrepreneurs around, capital is scarce or reserved for Elites, and there are few potential sources or customers. It's the difference between a jungle rich in nutrients and variation (recall that variation is information) and a sterile, lifeless desert.

8) Historian Fernand Braudel observed that concentrations of wealth, income, education and enterprise— in other words, cities—have always been higher-cost environments than the countryside or villages. Thus the cost basis of enterprise—the minimum revenues required to survive—will be higher in cities, but the income streams will be correspondingly larger.

If we analyze synergy and the higher cost basis of towns and cities, we find that some cities have high costs but do not offer the benefits of synergy. The ideal situation for new enterprise is a concentration of wealth, income, education and enterprise that offers the potential for resilient income streams that are multiples of the cost basis. In other words, if it costs $1,000 per month to be near a town that might support an income stream of $3,000 per month, that is attractive but not as attractive as a town which costs $2,000 to survive in but which offers the potential for multiple income streams totaling $10,000.

Put another way: merely living near high-synergy concentrations of wealth, income, education and enterprise offers tremendous leverage to the enterprising. This explains the continuing attraction of cities such as

London, Paris, Shanghai and San Francisco, and why cities have
attracted the ambitious and the wealthy for thousands of years. As I
have often noted on my website, great cities of hundreds of thousands of
people have been features of human society long before the discovery
and dependence on oil.

While many see cities as unsustainable in a Peak Oil era; perhaps
the more accurate assessment is that while today's energy-glutton cities
as currently configured are unsustainable, some are potentially more
sustainable than others. Urban centers exist because they enable
synergies and profits which are unattainable in low-density environments
devoid of synergies: America's 363 metropolitan areas hold 84% of the
population and generate 90% of the nation's GDP.

Cities enable social capital and novelty, two characteristics of wealth
that are not quantifiable but are nonetheless fundamental. As system
analyst Cesare Marchetti observed, "Intricate personal links and beauty
may be the most important components" of cities. Personal links is
another way of describing social capital, and "beauty" is another way of
describing novelty and variation—and since "variation is information," we
can also say that beauty and social capital are characteristics of
information-dense environments that breed synergies and adaptations.
Cities with these assets will attract capital and talent, those without them
will lose capital and talent.

The value of towns and cities can be illustrated by a simple example.
If you manufacture or reap a surplus of goods in a poor, sparsely
populated area, you will be unlikely to find enough buyers to soak up the
surplus. This lack of demand lowers the price, and you may not be able
to sell the surplus at a profit at all. If, however, you transport that surplus
to a city, then the concentration of demand—more people and more
wealth--will offer a much larger and more diverse market for your surplus.
That demand gives you pricing power you didn't have at home, and so
your profit margin rises. As long as transport costs are lower than the
pricing power gained, then it is advantageous to ship surplus to high-
demand locales. Transport costs are a much smaller part of the total

cost of goods than the production costs, and a rise in the cost of oil will not change this equation, as higher energy costs also raise the cost of production.

Towns and cities with high fixed costs and few trade-worthy natural assets such as harbors, rivers or nearby energy sources will likely experience wealth and income migrating to places which offer higher leverage. This is simply the result of the entrepreneurial imperative: move capital from low productivity to higher productivity.

Any locale which offers the leverage of synergy and an attractive balance of costs and potential income increases the value of an enterprise.

I am indebted to Bart Dessart and Eric Andrews for helping me understand the value of locally controlled, decentralized assets and enterprises.

19 | Hedging

A hedge is a way of insuring an investment: that is, a position specifically taken to offset potential losses in an asset exposed to risk.

Here is a simple example. In a coin toss, you bet $1 on heads. But since the odds are 50-50, you also place a $1 bet on tails. No matter what happens, you won't lose money.

In this hedge, you also can't make money. So there are two ideas in hedging: that the hedge protects you against loss but also allows you to make a profit if the trade goes the way you expected.

The classic hedge against stock market risk is an option: a call option leverages any increase in price and a put option gains value if price declines.

A simple example of a standard hedge will help illustrate the concept.

Let's say you own 100 shares of Global Widget Inc. which you bought for $50 per share because you expect the shares to double in value as others grasp the potential of the firm's products. Being a prudent and experienced investor, however, you know that shares could also fall in half is the company disappoints investors or if global markets crash. You could place a stop-loss sell order on the stock that would sell your position if the price falls below $45, and this would limit your loss to $5 per share. Or you could buy a put option as a hedge.

A put option rises in value as a stock falls in price. In a simplified version, if your 100 shares fell to $25 per share, you would lose $2,500. Since your one put option covers 100 shares, it will rise to $2,500 in value if Global Widget's shares fall to $25. So you lost $2,500 by owning 100 shares of Global Widget and made $2,500 by holding the put option hedge. As a result of your hedge, you lost nothing. The put option—your hedge—insured your investment against the horrendous loss of 50% of its value.

Options carry a specified price called the strike price, and they only perform their magic for a fixed period of time, at which point they expire worthless—the expiration date. As you might expect of something that acts like an insurance policy, options have a cost which varies with the risk being insured and the amount being insured.

Since there is a wealth of material available online and in other books on option trading, I will not cover the inner workings of an option contract here. The primary point is that options have an expiration date, after which they are worthless if price moved as you intended. In other words, if the shares of Global Widget rose to $60 by the time your put option expired, the put is worthless but you made $1,000 on your 100 shares. As long as the option cost less than $1,000, then you made a profit.

If the option cost $100, and your shares remain at $50 per share when the put expires, then the cost of "insuring" your 100 shares against major decline was $100.

Since hedges cost money, there is no perfect hedge; options expire and have to be repurchased. If the market stays flat then the costs incurred maintaining the hedge adds up. If you invest 5% of your portfolio in a hedge, and the market meanders around virtually unchanged, over three periods of hedging your portfolio declines 14.25%. Maintaining a hedge is not cost-free; it can lower your performance and erode value.

Even if the hedge works perfectly, all it did was keep your account from losing value. This raises the question: if all a hedge does is maintain the nominal value of your portfolio, then why be in a risky position that requires hedging? Why not be in cash, or some non-financial investment altogether?

A hedge deemed adequate to cover "typical" losses (i.e. those which reflect what has happened recently, not what could happen, which are two different sets of possibilities) may not cover the gargantuan losses of market meltdowns.

This is not to say hedging is not a good strategy. It is one method to manage risk. But the point here is that real risk can be much higher than *perceived risk*. That disparity is the key to understanding the cost of hedging.

Ironically, perhaps, hedging is "cheap" when perceived risk is low, and rapidly becomes "expensive" when the true nature of risk suddenly reveals itself. That sets up the peculiar dynamic that hedges look like a waste of money until risk unexpectedly pops up, at which point hedges become very costly.

In our example, put options on Global Widget shares are not infinite in number; they come into existence when an owner of Global Widget stock sells the put option on 100 of his shares. Thus options are subject to the same forces of supply and demand as any other liquid, marked-to-market asset: when the price of Global Widget shares starts plummeting, the value of the "insurance"—put options--rises, not just because they are more valuable but because there is now a speculative premium on the hedge.

Here is the Rule of Risk and Hedging: as the gap between perceived and real risk widens, the value of a hedge rises. Unfortunately, real risk is inherently unknowable for the reasons I have already explained, which means that hedges are priced on perceived risk and are thus open to mispricing. They are costly when real risk is visible and cheap just before crisis suddenly strikes, when perceived risk is low.

The ideal setting for a robust hedge is when the potential return is so promising that the risk-return is lopsided: the risk may be high, but the potential return is much higher. In that circumstance, the cost of hedging is commonsensical insurance against being wrong.

In other words, if the risk is such that you might lose half your position in a heartbeat, then hedging makes perfect sense. But exposing your capital to that kind of high risk makes no sense unless the potential return far outstrips the cost of the hedge.

This is the basic idea behind options strategies that take positions on both sides of the trade: straddles, collars, butterflies, strangles, and so on. (Do a Web search on these words if you want to learn more.)

Here's the problem with exposing your capital to any market: in "normal times," then the market fluctuations are modest, and thus the *perceived risk* is also modest. Mutual funds might rise or fall 5% over a few months, and such a modest variation is hardly worth hedging because the cost of the hedge limits the potential gain. If after paying for the hedge (including the commissions and management fees of a mutual fund or hedge fund) you earn a return of 1% or so, then what was the point of exposing your capital to risk in the first place?

But then along comes a sudden market collapse (which seem to be happening with greater frequency as the global markets become ever more intertwined and vulnerable to faraway catastrophes) and the investor finds the mutual fund has lost 40% of its value.

The perceived risk was low, but the actual risk was high.

How and when to hedge is already inherently difficult because true risk is impossible to assess, but to make matters worse the financial Status Quo actively seeks to cloak risk as part of its marketing strategy.

There is a third factor in hedging to consider. In the good old days before markets were so heavily manipulated into rising and falling together (what we call correlation), then you could hedge your position in bonds, say, by buying shares in a commodity fund such as the CRB (Commodities Research Bureau Fund). If inflation remained benign then your bonds would do well as interest rates declined, while if inflation and interest rates shot up, then commodities would tend to do well.

But since the Global Financial Meltdown bottomed in March 2009, all asset classes are moving as one trade: stocks are rising, bonds are rising, commodities are rising, precious metals are rising, oil is rising, bat guano is rising—every asset class under the sun is rising together, in opposition to the U.S. dollar, which sits on the other end of the global see-saw. As a result, the ability to hedge in a traditional sense by holding different asset classes is limited.

So hedging turns out to be filled with the same uncertainties and risks as the market itself.

Put another way: If trading and hedging were easy, then we'd all arrange 18 hedged high-risk, high-return trades in a row, reap a quick million and be high-fiving each other in swank celebration.

Futures Contracts Hedging

My trading mentor Harun once summarized the principles of hedging in this fashion:

"From what I understand about hedging, it does not matter when one buys or sells. What is needed is an understanding of risk and consciously seeking ways of mitigating the known risks. For example, a farmer must raise and sell his crops. What the market price will be at harvest is unknowable and out of his control. The airline must fly but has no control over fuel prices it must purchase to conduct business. In neither instance is it practical to shut down business until prices become optimal. Since future price is unknowable, what price is optimal? And since crop and flights could not be brought into being instantly, how could we take advantage of the optimal price when it materialized?

The only constant is uncertainty. Learning to manage risk as a producer, consumer or both should be the endeavor.

Since the future is unknown there is no 'perfect' time to purchase or sell anything. There is only risk. If one happened to get the highest or lowest price it occurred by chance.

We are immersed in a sea of risk as a function of our existence; however, few give conscious thought to this and therefore take no conscious steps to manage important risks. This failure to live consciously is how government grows and becomes more tyrannical."

In very simple terms, we might observe the risk of wheat rising in price due to droughts in wheat-growing regions, and in response buy bulk bags of flour while it is still inexpensive (storing them in secure containers, of course). If wheat rises in price, we can consume our cheap flour at a discount to market prices. If wheat does not rise in price, the cost of our hedge-- storing 100 pounds of flour--is relatively modest.

If gasoline and natural gas are currently inexpensive compared to recent tops, then we might purchase a futures contract on gasoline or natural gas which serves to protect us against future spikes in price.

The value of the futures contract (which can be purchased at various broker/dealers much like stocks or options, with some restrictions and requirements) varies depending on the current price of the contract month of the commodity being hedged. But just for purposes of illustration, let's suppose a futures contract on gasoline costs $1,000 and the household consumes $3,000 of gasoline a year.

The total cost of the gasoline and the hedge is thus $4,000. If gasoline drops in price, then the hedge--essentially a bet that gasoline would rise in price--loses value. So if gasoline drops such that the family only consumes $2,000 a year, then the household budget remains $3,000--the gasoline cost of $2,000 plus the $1,000 cost of the futures contract hedge.

But if gasoline rises dramatically in cost, then the futures contract might well climb to $4,000. Since fuel prices jumped, the cost of the family's gasoline consumption might rise to $5,000 a year. But since their hedge rose in value as gasoline rose in price, the household can sell the futures contract for a profit of $4,000 (if the trade works, the initial $1,000, which is a performance bond, is returned at liquidation). Thanks to the hedge, the net cost of the family's gasoline is only $1,000 ($5,000 gasoline cost minus profit from hedge $4,000 = $1,000).

Thus the purchase of the hedge lowered the family's total gasoline expenses to $1,000 for the year--a savings of $4,000.

As Harun noted, agricultural and transport enterprises hedge against fluctuations in their cost of goods with futures contracts, and global enterprises also hedge against fluctuations in currencies.

While this example might seem complex, the underlying strategy is simple: by investing in a futures hedge, risks can be offset or reduced.

Hedging Income and Assets

If a household depends entirely on one income source (one wage earner), then the risk of that wage earner losing their job could be partially offset or reduced by developing an alternate source of income or by buying a "loss of income" insurance policy.

Developing multiple sources of revenue is a form of hedging against the risk of the household losing its sole source of income. This might mean another household member seeks a part-time job, a spare room is rented to a student, a garden is planted in Spring and the produce sold at farmer's markets, a new skill is acquired by someone in the household and marketed through friends, family and other networks, a small-scale Internet-based enterprise is developed, etc.

There is no one answer to how to offset or mitigate risk, but having multiple sources of essentials, rigorous cost controls and carefully planned hedges against potential catastrophes is a strategy with a much higher probability of success than remaining passively exposed to foreseeable risks.

All of these concepts are simply forms of risk management. We cannot make risk vanish, but we can hedge against contingencies.

A futures contract is ultimately based on a real commodity, and the last owner of that contract has the right to take physical delivery of the underlying commodity. Due to the high cost of storage, few investors do so. But this raises another hedging option for those with inexpensive storage: stockpiling commodities when they are cheap, and selling them when they become fully valued. While commodities such as gasoline have shelf-lives and hazards of storage to consider, others such as canned coffee and refined sugar have long shelf-lives and few hazards of storage.

Just as the spectra of capital and enterprise are broad, so too is the range of hedging options.

Gold as a Hedge

Just as a thought experiment, let's ask: how much gold would be needed as a prudent hedge against the depreciation of fiat currencies? The starting point assumption: there is some probability (low or high is a matter of judgment) that as a result of the fundamental imbalances in the current global financial system, fiat currencies will lose most of their purchasing power. This is also referred to as hyperinflation or loss of faith in paper money.

Some observers have made the case that this is not a probability but the inevitable end-game of the Status Quo, and that the only practical choice as a replacement for debased paper currencies is a gold-backed currency—a topic mentioned previously.

You don't have to judge this as likely to consider a hedge; you simply have to assess it as a possibility.

How much gold would a household need to hedge their paper wealth against depreciation? In his paper *Apropos of Everything*, Paul Brodsky reckoned that gold at $10,000 an ounce would enable the U.S. to back its current money supply with the 256 million ounces of gold it holds in reserve.

That is one rough approximation of how much gold one would need to hold to hedge paper financial assets. If gold were to rise 6.6-fold from $1,500 to $10,000, then $10,000 of gold at today's price (6.6 ounces in US dollars) would hedge $66,000 in paper financial capital.

In other words, if the dollar (and other paper currencies) fell into the inflationary black hole and disappeared over the event horizon, then the 6.6 ounces of gold would be equal in purchasing power to the $66,000 in paper assets that just vanished.

There are of course many other complicating factors, but this is a rough calculation.

If we follow the idea presented by Brodsky that gold-backed money would have to equal all the current paper money, then our thought experiment would start with the current financial net worth (assets minus liabilities) in the U.S. which according to the Fed Flow of Funds is about $35 trillion. (Net fixed assets such as real estate are about $10 trillion.)

Total financial assets are $47 trillion, but these include corporate equities and non-corporate business assets which include factories, production facilities, etc. owned by the corporate and non-corporate enterprises. These tangible assets would still retain their utility value after the "event horizon" depreciation, so they should be deducted to leave purely paper financial assets such as stocks and bonds.

If you disagree, then adjust the financial assets down to whatever number you think approximates the financial wealth that would be lost in a stick/slip "black hole" currency depreciation.

The U.S. has about 25% of the world's wealth, so let's multiply the $35 trillion in purely financial capital by four: thus the global economy has about $140 trillion in purely financial wealth.

This is a very rough back-of-the-envelope guesstimate.

There are about 5.3 billion ounces of gold "above ground," roughly 160,000 tons. At the current price of about $1,500 an ounce, all the available gold is worth about $8 trillion. About half is in jewelry, 10% in industrial uses and 40% as central bank reserves and investment.

If gold took the place of fiat currencies as "money," the available gold would have to rise to about $140 trillion in value. In today's dollars, that's about 18 times its current price. So $1,500 X 18 = $27,000 an ounce.

Let's round that off to $25,000 an ounce. (Feel free to round it up to $30,000 if you prefer.) If you prefer to subtract industrial gold or other uses from the calculation, then the number will be much higher. I am presenting the idea as simply as possible.

In this thought experiment, ten ounces of gold, or $15,000 worth at today's prices would hedge $250,000 in paper financial wealth (recall that productive real estate, windmills, factories, etc. would still retain their utility value after currency depreciation).

Though we cannot be sure anything about the future, we can be reasonably certain that gold will not go to zero value, since it will likely retain its industrial and decorative value. Thus owning gold is not like owning a hedge (such as an option) which expires. Gold does not need to be "renewed," so it is a unique insurance.

Let's say massive fiat currency depreciation never occurs, and instead gold falls 50% in dollar-denominated value to $750/ounce. Many consider this impossible, just as others think a loss of faith in the dollar is a near-impossibility. Both are possibilities, regardless of the odds anyone places on them at any one moment in time.

If gold falls in half to $750, then the gold hedge against destruction of paper money would have cost $7,500, in opportunity cost if nothing else. That's a relatively modest price for $250,000 of "portfolio insurance" via a hedge that doesn't expire.

If gold is confiscated, the Central State might follow the 1933 model of allowing five ounces of private gold per citizen. As we have seen, five ounces per person (or ten ounces for a two-person household) would still offer a very useful hedge. (Private gold could also be transferred to a safe-haven nation while such a transfer remains legal, though this introduces a new set of risks and costs.)

To complete the thought experiment: it doesn't really matter if the "new dollar" or bancor that replaces the discredited currency is backed by gold or not; it might be a "hard currency" based on some other scheme. The point is that if the present currencies suffer significant depreciation, then gold will reflect that.

In other words, if one "new dollar" replaces 20 devalued 2011 dollars, then gold will be worth 20 X $1,500 or $30,000 an ounce when the "new dollar" is imposed. Gold needn't be the "official money" at all to act as money.

Nobody knows what will happen, tomorrow or next year or five years from now--to the price of gold in dollars, to the value of dollars in other currencies, or anything else. This thought experiment is an exploration of hedging, not a speculation on the future price of anything.

Concluding Thoughts

You have now completed the long and hopefully thought-provoking journey through this book. If there is one idea I hope you have embraced, it is that no one else can possibly be qualified to make decisions on how best to invest your human, social and financial capital. The only person qualified to do so is you.

Since investing human, social and financial capital is ultimately a form of self-expression, there are no "right answers" or easy answers. Rather, there is only risk, opportunity and contingency—the unknown, the ambiguous, the changeable.

Charles Hugh Smith
July 20, 2011
Berkeley California, U.S.A.

Made in the USA
Lexington, KY
10 December 2011